A DAY IN KĀSHĪ

A DAY IN KĀSHĪ

Photographs by Séverine DABADIE

Text written by Christiane ETCHEZAHARRETA
Séverine DABADIE

Translated from the French by David Azpiazu Torres

PILGRIMS PUBLISHING
◆ Varanasi ◆

A DAY IN KĀSHĪ
Photographs by Séverine DABADIE
Text written by Christiane ETCHEZAHARRETA
Séverine DABADIE

Published by:
PILGRIMS PUBLISHING

An imprint of:
PILGRIMS BOOK HOUSE
(Distributors in India)
B 27/98 A-8, Nawabganj Road
Durga Kund, Varanasi-221010, India
Tel: 91-542- 2314060, 2312456
E-mail: pilgrims@satyam.net.in
Website: www.pilgrimsbooks.com

PILGRIMS BOOK HOUSE (New Delhi)
9 Netaji Subhash Marg, 2nd Floor
Near Neeru Hotel, Daryaganj, New Delhi 110002
Tel: 91-11-23285081 Fax: 91-11-23285722
E-mail: pilgrim@del2.vsnl.net.in

Cover Photograph by Séverine DABADIE
Edited by Christopher N Burchett
Layout by Asha Mishra

ISBN: Franch 81-7769-387-5   English 81-7769-388-3

Printed in India at Pilgrim Press Pvt. Ltd. Lalpur Varanasi

TO ALL BANĀRSĪS

We thank sincerely the following people for their loving and precious help: Shree Rajendra Kumar Dūbe (Bablu), Babaji Shibananda, Vanesa García Cazorla, and Krishna Kant Shukla.

We also address our warmest thanks for the support and the trust of: Rama Nand Tiwari, Christopher N. Burchett, Asha Mishra.

We would also like to thank Dr. Rana P. B. Singh for his kind permission allowing us to use some of his wonderful maps and illustrations.

"If there is a place on the earth where all dreams of the living men have found a house from the most ancient times, where the man began the dream of the existence, it is certainly India."

Romain Rolland.

INTRODUCTION

Kāshī is the original name of this more than 3000 years old mythical and mystical city. It is also known by the names of Vārānasī or Banāras. The former is its most explicit, most beautiful and most poetic name: Kāshī, the city of light. The meaning of the word Kāshī is: "concentration of the cosmic light". This name is to be found, in texts from the 15th century BC: "Kāshī shines and illuminates the universe. Kāshī covers everyone with Moksha (liberation) and gives wisdom." Atharva Veda (V.22.4). That is Kāshī, the Luminous one.

The name Vārānasī comes from the two tributaries of the Ganges, Varanā and Asi, it is located between the confluences of both. The legend says that Varanā and Asi would be, the right and left leg of Vishnu respectively. It has been the administrative name of the city since May 24, 1956.

It is also known by the name of Banāras, a corrupted form of Vārānasī or, according to some, "Bana": always ready, and "Ras": juice of life, which would mean (according to the etymology) that Banāras would be the city where the juice of the life would be always ready.

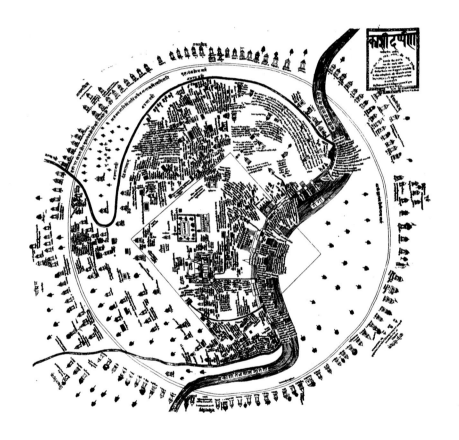

It was also called Avimukta in the old texts. It means "never abandoned", in reference to the fact that it never stopped being a living city, inhabited for over 3 000 years, which confers it the honour of being one of the oldest cities in the world, along with Beijing, Jerusalem

1

Alexandria and Athens. It also received other names such as: Ānandavana: the forest of happiness, Rudravāsa: Shiva's city or Mahāshmashāna: the great place of cremation, since more than 38 000 bodies are cremated there each year.

Vārānasī—this is the way by which it has to be officially referred to—is an important city in the Indian State of Uttar Pradesh, located 80 meters above sea level and some 120 kilometres to the east of Allāhābad (Prayāga) famous for the Khumbha Melā. The city has a population of more than 1.5 million inhabitants for an area of 74 km².

It is spread along the left bank of River Ganges, facing the rising sun and is the only place where the river flows northwards. This city is also called the city of the God Shiva but, above all, the city of light. It is on the banks of the Ganges, which provides it with the energy of a mystical flood.

Kāshī—as we prefer to name it since it is its original name—is the place of all prayers, but it is also, itself, a prayer. It represents the city of Hinduism par excellence, and the Holy City where all Hindus dream to make their pilgrimage (Yātrā) to, wish to die and to be cremated. Dying in Banāras, having your ashes thrown into the holy river is the ultimate wish of each Hindu, as it means reaching the Moksha, the release, i.e. the end of the cycle of reincarnations, known as samsāra. Kāshī is fundamentally a deeply mystic city. But even if the city is recognised by all Hindus as one of the best places to die, it should not be forgotten that the Banārsīs cherish there a style of living they are certainly committed to. It is a city where life, death and eternity mix together. This feeling is perceptible in the innermost recesses of the city. Banāras is not only a town of culture, it is the culture itself, this is why this city of more than one million and half inhabitants is not easy to grasp and understand. It is one of the world's oldest inhabited cities. In spite of time, several violent invasions by the Mughals, and a history agitated by the upheavals of time, it never stopped being a lively and animated town. It survived all the disturbances, the repeated invasions and the looting of the temples that were the soul of the city. As recounted in the Kāshī Khanda (35.10): "The River Ganges, Lord Shiva and the divine city of Kāshī are the trinity of grace and perfect happiness". The holy river, which bathes it, gives it this vital energy and its mystical power.

But Kāshī is also the city of Knowledge. It has always attracted intellectuals from everywhere. There are more than 50 schools still teaching the Sanskrit language, more than six large schools, as well as the largest Indian university, the celebrated Banāres Hindu University where knowledge is spread to thousands of students coming

not only from the whole of India, but also from abroad. In the 6th century BC, the Buddha himself was attracted to the town of light.

Kāshī is also the residence of Shiva and attracts millions of pilgrims each year. Each day, more than 20,000 people make their morning ablutions along the Gange's stairs known here as "ghāts". On special occasions (during important festivals) it is possible to find more than one million devotees bathing in the Ganges. There are more than 3,000 temples and other Hindu places of worship in the city. There are also 1,400 mosques or Muslim worship places, twelve churches, three Jain temples, nine Buddhist temples (Vihara) and three Sikh temples (Gurudwara). But—as it is often forgotten—it is also a trading town. Banāras, Kāshī or Vārānasī (no matter which one of these three names are chosen to call it) is more than a city. It is, itself, a significant part of the soul and vital energy of the country. It is one of the essential sites that allows one to discover the mysteries of India.

HISTORY

The civilisation in the valley of the Indus (2600 BC-1500 BC), was one from the Ancient World whose geographical area spread mainly along the Indus river, in the Indian sub-continent. It is not known what influence it could have had on the contemporary Hindu culture. Forgotten by History until its rediscovery in the 1920s, the Indus' civilisation stands among its contemporary civilisations (Mesopotamia and ancient Egypt) as one of the very first civilisations, defined as such by the establishment of cities, agriculture, and writing, etc.

Although the Indus civilisation is not the most ancient one, (because Mesopotamia, as well as Egypt had cities before), it is however the one that covers the greatest geographical territory. In its apogee, its population could have exceeded five million people. It was an urban civilisation: there were two main cities (Mohenjo Daro and Harappa).

Despite all these achievements, this civilisation is hardly known. Its very existence remained forgotten even until the 20th century. Its writing has already been deciphered, and it is not known if it has any link at all with the Brahmi writing, which seems unlikely nowadays. Among the mysteries it holds, there are at least two fundamental questions:

What were its means of subsistence?

Which are the causes of its sudden and dramatic extinction, from 1900 BC onwards?

We do not know which language was spoken (maybe a Dravidian language?), nor the names by which they called themselves.

The connections between the Indus civilisation and the first Sanskrit culture, which produced the Vedic texts of Hinduism, are not clear. However, the oldest Vedic texts mention the Sarasvatī River and describe a world close to Utopia, which lived on its banks. The latest texts refer, however, to its extinction.

Are these texts only depicting a myth?

However, as many archaeologists noticed, there is something inexplicably "Indian" in the Indus' civilisation. On the basis of the large quantity of figurines representing female fertility they have passed on to us, the people of this civilisation seem to have worshiped some sort of mother goddess found in contemporary Hinduism (Shakti and Kālī). Their seals depict animals in a manner that suggests veneration, leading us to predict the future sacred character that the Hindus allocate to cows and other animals, like the monkey, for example. Like today's Hindus, they seem to have given great importance to ablutions and body hygiene. The Indian figurines adopt the posture of the yogis, legs crossed, suggesting that yoga or meditation was one their practices. There are figurines of lingam and yoni (symbolic representations of both the male and the female sexual organs), which are still widespread today in the popular forms of Shiva's worship. As opposed to other ancient civilisations, archaeological research does not highlight here the presence of any powerful leaders, vast armies, slaves, social conflicts, prisons and any other aspects usually related to the first civilisations. However, these gaps may also be the result of our very limited knowledge about this civilisation.

The end of the Indus' civilisation, circa 1800 BC, was explained through the sudden arrival of invaders coming from the North West, which would have constituted the first wave of Aryan migration.

The Aryans were nomads living on animal husbandry and agriculture. The "Aryan" word comes from the Sanskrit and from the vestic term āryā (language of Avesta, a collection of holy writings of the mazdean religion (ancient Iran), which means "noble". They invaded India circa 2000 BC, and gradually conquered it. At that time, their centre was an area located between Yamunā and Satlaj and the higher course of the Sarasvatī. The Ganges is only mentioned once.

It is during the Vedic age, that the Aryan society divided itself into four parts (Varna) the Brahmans (priests), Kshatriyas (warriors), Vaishyas (farmers and businessmen), and Shudras (servant). It is generally thought that these groups—Varnas (colours in Sanskrit)—were formed as a result of the Aryan tribes interacting with the indigenous populations. The family constituted the basic cell of society. The village is often described as the regrouping of a lineage rather than as a territorial regrouping. The family was patriarchal. The woman was submissive to her husband and marriages were indissoluble. The horse was as important as the cow because of its military use.

On a political level, the Aryans set up tribal monarchies to be ruled by the Rājā. He did not exert an absolute power and shared the sovereignty with two tribal councils: Sabhā and Samiti.

KĀSHĪ: ITS HISTORY

Although tradition dates it back up to 2000 years BC, the town of Kāshī was probably founded in the 7th century BC, which makes it one of the world's oldest permanently inhabited cities. An ancient centre for religious studies, it was on its outskirts, in Sarnāth (then known as 'Rishipatana' or 'Issipatana'), where the Buddha gave his first sermon after his enlightenment in Bodhgayā. The city is quoted in the both Hindu epics, 'The Mahābhārata' and 'The Rāmāyana'.

Being seen as an important symbol of Hinduism, it was looted and destroyed several times by the Muslim invaders, the first time by the Ghazni Mahmud's army in 1033. Its temples were destroyed, and the materials re-used to build mosques; the last destruction campaign being carried out by the Mughal emperor Aurangzeb (1658-1707), who renamed the city as Mohammadābād and ordered the destruction of more than a thousand temples. The city eventually came under British control in 1775.

Because of its violent and eventful history, there are not many old monuments remaining, but this does not prevent the city from keeping its sacred status and its dominating position in Hindu society.

The town of Vārānasī is particularly famous for its ghāts, (banks covered with stone steps), which allow the Hindu devotees to descend to the river to practise their ablutions and pūjās. Having a bath in the Ganges is supposed to wash away all sins and therefore to be released from the cycle of rebirths. It is also on the ghāts—the most popular one known as Manikarnikā—where cremations take place. Jai Singh II of Jaipur built (around 1740) one of his five observatories, overhanging the Man Mandir ghāt.

The most important temple of the city is Vishvanāth Mandir (or golden temple). It was built in the 10th century and was several times destroyed and even replaced by a mosque. The current temple, built from 1750 to 1777, thanks to the efforts of the queen Ahilyā Bāī, replaces the one that was destroyed by Aurangzeb. Entrance is banned to non-Hindus.

HINDUISM

Hinduism is one of the oldest of the world's religions. Hinduism, or more appropriately, Sanātana Dharma (eternal religion), is a way of living and thinking rather than an organized religion. Historically, "Hindu" does not refer to a system of religious beliefs. The term, of a Persian origin, refers to the people who live on the other side (from a Persian point of view) of Sind, on the banks of the Indus. After the British colonization, the term was used to indicate a not well-defined set of religious aspects. In 1966, the Supreme Court of India defined the scope of the Hindu faith as follows: the acceptance of the Veda as a Higher Authority on the religious and philosophical matters and the acceptance of the Veda by the Hindu thinkers and philosophers as the only basis of their philosophy, the spirit of tolerance and goodwill in order to understand and appreciate the point of view of the adversary, based on the revelation that the truth appears in different forms, the acceptance by all of the six Hindu philosophical systems of a rhythm of the world which has periods of creation, maintenance and destruction, periods (or Yuga) that follow one another endlessly, the acceptance by all the Hindu philosophical systems of the belief in the rebirth and the pre-existence of entities, becoming aware of the fact that there are several means or ways to achieve redemption, understanding the truth that, however large the number of divinities to be adored may be, one can however be Hindu and not believe in the need to worship idols. Unlike other Faiths or religions, Hinduism is not related to a definite body of philosophical concepts.

The Hindu religion shows a remarkable syncretism, conciliating a great number of beliefs and practices. It involves all the aspects of the human life and is not reduced to a simple ideology. The daily actions are more determining than the beliefs. Almost all Hindus worship Shiva and Vishnu, and at the same time hundreds, maybe even millions of other minor deities that can belong specifically to a specific village, a family or clan. The respect for the Brahmans and the cows, a pure (sattvic) diet and the avoidance of eating meat especially beef, marriages within the same caste and the importance of the male heirs are the only principles that achieve unanimity. Hindus believe the Universe to be a large closed sphere, a cosmic egg inside of which paradises, hell, concentric oceans -as well as the continents with India in the centre- are found. Life is also cyclic: after death, the soul (*atma*) passes to a new body, be it human, animal, vegetable or mineral. This uninterrupted process of death and rebirth is called samsāra. The karma is a principle of the Hindu philosophy. It consists in the sum of all the acts, good or bad, setting up the conditions for the transmigrations of the soul over its successive incarnations. It is possible to counterweight its effects by behaving justly and disinterestedly, via rituals, or via expiatory practices and hence to be released from the cycle of birth and death (Moksha). The Hindus cremate their dead ones because fire purifies. Being cremated in Kāshī and having one's ashes thrown in the Ganges, releases one from the cycle of rebirths.

During their lifetime, Hindus must settle three debts: the study of the Vedas (owed to wise men), the delivery of a son (owed to the ancestors) and the sacrifices (owed to the gods).

Due to the social foundations, Hinduism implies ceremonies every Hindu takes part in, and which are mainly rites of transitions (samskāra). The several stages include: the birth, the day the child eats solid food (rice) for the first time, the day -at the age of two- they have their first haircut, the wearing of the sacred thread (janeū) the purification of the girl after her first menstruation, the marriage…Pregnancy—and subsequently the childbirth—are blessed in a number of rituals. Finally, there are the funerary ceremonies (the cremation and whenever possible the ashes' disposal in a holy river, such as the Ganges or any of its tributaries), and the annual offerings to the ancestors (shrāddha). Daily rituals involve ceremonies (pūjās) and offerings (prasād) of fruit, rice and flowers. The one in charge is usually the woman, because she is considered to be more capable of interceding with the gods. The temple is a cultural place where one sings, reads sacred texts aloud, carries out the rites at sunset. There are thousands of small local temples. Some are barely a small stone cavity containing an effigy—with no precise shape—wrapped in any fabric, or a slightly more imposing building with a small basin for ablutions.

RELIGIOUS TEXTS

VEDAS

A Hindu is defined as one who believes in the phi losophy contained in the Vedas (knowledge). The Vedas are perhaps one of the oldest religious writings in the world. The Vedic religion was introduced by the Aryans when they invaded the North-West of India, between 2000 and 1500 B.C. They would thus have a double origin: Indo-Iranian and Indo-European. As the result of a fast evolution and of the interaction with the natives, the ancient forms enriched or deteriorated. The basic teaching of Vedas is that the true human nature is divine. God—or Brahman—exists in each living being. Religion is thus a search for one's self, a search for the divine presence in each individual. The Vedas state that nobody needs "to be saved", for nobody ever gets lost. In the worst cases, one lives in ignorance of his true divine nature.

First of all, the ideas expressed in the Vedas were traditionally transmitted orally from father to child and from teacher to pupil. Later on, these ideas (that had

been around for a long time) were codified and compiled by a wise man named Vyāsa (literally, "the compiler").

Researchers have mentioned various dates for the origin of the Vedas—approximately from 5000 BC to 1500 BC.

In the Hindu traditional conception, the Vedas would have no beginning nor end, which means that the truths described in these writings are eternal and rather than created by the human spirit. This is what makes them different to the teachings of Buddhism and Jaļnism. There are four Vedas: Rig-veda, Yajur-veda, Sāma-veda and later the Atharva-veda.

The vedic religion, especially in ancient times, had several aspects that made it different to the current practice of Hinduism, in particular the reference to women as religious authorities, featuring the existence of women rishis (wise), an apparent lack of belief in the reincarnation, and a definitely different Pantheon, with Indra as the head of the gods. The trinity of Brahmā, Vishnu, and Shiva is rarely mentioned.

UPANISHAD OR "APPROACHES"

Being a body of inspired teachings, visions and mystic experiments led by India's old wise men, the Upanishad represent commentateries and explanations of the Vedas. Through a vast variety of forms and styles, all these writings (including the 108 main ones) deliver the same basic teaching: the individual soul and God are one.

VEDĀNTA

Vedānta is based on the Vedas and their teaching, and more specifically on the Upanishad. The philosophy of the Vedānta asserts the unity of the world, the identity of the individual conscience and the universal conscience. It recognizes that there are many different approaches to God, and that all of them are valid. Any kind of spiritual practice leads to the same state of self-fulfilment. Thus, the Vedānta teaches respect for all beliefs and is set apart from most of the other main religions by strongly encouraging tolerance towards these different creeds and systems.

Hinduism exists today on two different levels; the first one based purely on the faith and the second one is based on philosophy. Often these two levels intertwine.

GODS

There are three main gods in the Hindu Pantheon - which accounts for some 330 millions: Brahmā, Vishnu and Shiva. The Brahmā god symbolizes the creator, Vishnu represents the preserver and Shiva represents the destroyer in the cycle of the existence.

Vaishnava (worshipers of Vishnu), currently around an 80 % of all Hindus, adore one of the two most recent avatars—or terrestrial incarnations—of Vishnu as their main deity; The seventh avatar of Vishnu, Lord Rāmā, and the eighth, Lord Krishna. Most of the remaining 20% of the Hindus are Shivaïtes, who adore Shiva. The rest are devoted to Shakti, Ishvara or the obscure goddess Kālī.

BRAHMĀ

In the Hindu religion, Brahmā is the creative god, the first member of the Trimūrti, the trinity of the major Hindu deities—the other members being Vishnu and Shiva. The Goddess Sarasvatī is his shakti, his energy, his wife. His vehicle (vāhana), namely his animal means of transport, is Hamsa, a goose or a swan. His colour is red. He is not mentioned in the Veda, nor in the Brāhmana, but he is however very present in the Mahābhārata, the Rāmāyana and the Purāna. Brahmā intervenes only occasionally in the gods' affairs, and even more rarely in those of the mortals. Brahmā lives in Brahmāpura, a city located on mount Meru.

REPRESENTATION OR MŪRTI

He is traditionally represented with four heads and four arms. Each one of his heads recites one of the four Vedas. Often, the reliefs below the main images show only three of them. According to the legend Shiva would have cut one of them. His hands hold a nozzle pot used to create life, a mālā (rosary) to measure the time of the universe, the Veda texts and a lotus flower (kamal).

His four heads are explained in the following legend: when he was creating the universe, Brahmā begot a female deity named Shatarūpā, the one with a hundred beautiful shapes. Brahmā fell immediately in love with her. Shatarūpā moved consequently in many directions to avoid the ogling of Brahmā. But, wherever she went, Brahmā created for himself a new head so that he could continue to stare at her. In the end, he had five of them, one for each cardinal direction and one to look above. In order to control Brahmā, Shiva cut his higher head. But when he found out that Shatarūpā was Brahmā's daughter, he decided that it was improper for Brahmā to be obsessed with her and ruled that there would be no place where Brahmā should be venerated. Indeed, only Vishnu (or his avatars) and Shiva continue to be worshiped, whereas Brahmā is almost completely ignored. He has only one temple dedicated to him, in Pushkar. Ever since this incident happened, Brahmā recites the four Veda as penitence.

SHIVA

Shiva (sanskrit Śiva) transcribed sometimes as Siva, "the good, the nice one", is a Hindu god, an element of the Trimūrti, the "Hindu trinity". Shiva is not mentioned by name in the Vedas but the representation of Rudra has later been accepted as a representation of Shiva. In the Trimūrti, Shiva is the destroyer, whereas Brahmā and Vishnu are respectively the creator and the preserver. However, although he represents destruction, he is regarded as a positive force, since, after destruction, regenerative creation follows. Besides, he saves the world on at least two occasions: when he intercedes between the earth and the feet of Kālī (she is furious after having been defeated by him in a Bharata Natyam competition), and then during the churning of the "Ocean Milk" when he swallows the goblet of poison that is produced, poison which leaves him with a blue mark on the throat.

Shiva is the inner fire that devours the ascetics, the time that destroys and recreates the world. He is usually represented by a stylised phallus, called Shiva lingam, a symbol of creation sometimes linked to the yoni, the female organ, the world's matrix. His residence is Mount Kailash (Kailāsa) and his vehicle (vāhana in Sanskrit) is a white bull, called Nandī (merry) or Nandikeshvara (Lord-of-the-joy). The wife of Shiva, his Shakti (śakti), appears in several shapes: Pārvatī (the girl of the Himalayas), Durgā (the inaccessible one), Kālī (the goddess of death). Shiva was also married to Satī, Daksha's daughter, who was opposed to their marriage. But please note that all of these represent Pārvatī in her different forms.

His worshippers, the shivaites, regard him as the only creator. Shivaism is one of the two main branches of today's Hinduism, the other one being the vaishnavism.

Shiva and Pārvatī are the parents of Skanda and Ganesh, the elephant god, who removes the obstacles. Traditionally—and unlike Vishnu—Shiva does not have avatars.

REPRESENTATION OR MŪRTI

Among Shiva's attributes, we find the following:

Ganges: it runs from the crown of his untidy hair. It purifies everything.

His matted hair jatā, where his ascetic powers are based.

The third eye, (the frontal eye, closed, the eye of fire), looking inside, because when it opens, its glance burns what is in front of him.

The four arms symbol of the universal domination, they represent the four spatial directions, epitomising the control over the elements.

The trident (trīshul): it symbolizes the three fundamental functions of nature (creator, preserver, and destroyer).

The spear (pāshupata): Shiva's favourite weapon.

The axe (parashu): combat weapon.

The bow (pināka): weapon used to help the gods.

The bludgeon (khatvānga): bludgeon decorated with a dead head.

The lace he binds the refractory culprits with.

The necklace of dead heads represents the never-ending cycle of the ages.

The ashes (vibhūti) recall that Shiva reduced the Universe and all the gods to ashes. Then, he coated his body with them.

The drum of sand glass (damaru).

The crescent of the moon, diadem he bears on his forehead, close to the third eye.

The cobra, Kundalinī, source of sexual and mental power.

A tiger skin, symbolizing his control over Nature's power.

The bull

The lion

As an ascetic but also as the Lord of the Cremation Ground, Shiva covers his body with ash. He protects the earth from the force of the Ganges. He calms down the fierceness of its streams by filtering them through his curls. He often carries a conch in one of his hands and has a trident, a symbol that comprises—for his devotees—the powers of the Trimūrti, that is, creation, perpetuation and destruction. According to the legend, Shiva and Vishnu went into a forest to fight 10,000 heretics. Furious, they sent a tiger, a snake and a black

and wild dwarf, armed with a bludgeon, to attack Shiva. Shiva killed the tiger (he thus traditionally sits on a tiger's skin, as the master of Nature), he tamed the snake and wore it around his neck as a necklace, placed his foot on top of the dwarf and performed a dance which generated such a power, that the dwarf and the heretics recognized him as their Lord.

VARIOUS NAMES OF SHIVA

Shiva has many names such as Chandrashekhara, the moon in the hair, Gangādhara, Ganges bearer, Girīsha, the lord of the mountain, Ishāna, Lord, Kalā, the Time, Kapālamalin, bearer of skulls, Pashupati, Master of the herds, Nātarāja, king of the dance, Mahesh, Great Lord, Triambaka, the One with the three eyes, Nīlakantha, the One with the blue neck, Yogarāja, the king of yoga, Mahāyogi, the Great Yogi, Shankara, the provider of luck, Bhagavata, the Divine One, Bhairava, the terrible One, Vishvanātha, the lord of All Things, etc.

VISHNU

Vishnu, also known as Hari, is a Hindu god associated with conservation and protection. He is the second god of the Trimūrti (also called the Hindu trinity), with Brahmā and Shiva. It is a divinity of life-death-rebirth.

Vishnu is often depicted as sitting or resting on a lotus (Kamal). His wife is Lakshmī, the goddess of wealth and of good fortune; her vehicle is called Garuda, the eagle.

REPRESENTATION OR MŪRTI

The conch is the symbol of creation; its internal spiral represents expansion. The sound it produces is the image of the fundamental sound.

The Sudarshana disc (pleasant to look at) comprises of six rays like the six petals of the lotus flower. It symbolizes the power of the spirit, the power of the mind.

The lotus symbolizes the display of creation, but also the purity.

The bow is the instrument we use to launch the waves of intuition into the unknown spheres of an illusory creation.

The arrows and the quiver: the power of the senses, the field of the intellect, and the power of action.

The bludgeon: the power of knowledge from which all the other powers originate, physical or intellectual.

The Treasure of the Ocean jewel or Kausthubha, which shines on the chest of the god: the universal conscience made out of the consciences of all beings.

The Dear-to-the-fortune tuft of hair or Shrī-vasta, located above the left breast of the god, that represents everything the conscience can endeavour.

The Garland of the forest or vana, mālā is the image of Māyā, the illusion.

The two earrings represent the two ways towards the knowledge, Sānkhya, the intellectual one and yoga, the intuitive one. They take the shape of Makara, a sea monster.

The bracelets symbolize the three goals in life: self-fulfilment, success, pleasure.

The crown: the unknowable reality.

The yellow veil or pītāmbara, worn around the waist, represents the Vedas.

The sacred cord: composed of three bits, the three letters from the AUM syllable.

The carriage represents the mind and its power of action over the world.

The dark colours: colours of Immanence, of the ether, of the space's substance.

The flyswatter, symbol of the dharma (order, duty, laws, uprightness, religious duties, rites, religious tradition).

The fan represents the sacrifice; it is used to poke the flames.

The flag: "the glory of the sun and the moon".

The parasol, symbol of the god's royalty, its pole being the world's axis, mount Meru.

The sword and the sheath symbolize the knowledge and the ignorance, which covers it.

Garuda: half vulture, half man, vehicle of Vishnu.

The Vestige snake or Shesha Nāga: the one on top of which the god rests when he sleeps, awaiting the Creation.

THE GANGES

It is in Garhwal, a mountain massif in the Himalayas where the Ganges originates. The Ganges is an important river (its length varies depending on the sources from 2,500 to 3,000 km). Its basin covers 2,165 000 km² and its delta, shared with the Brahmaputra, covers 110 000 km². The Ganges is the holiest of India's seven holy rivers.

One of its most famous sources flows from the Gangotrī glacier at 6 600 m above sea level in the Himalayas, where it is known as Bhagīrathī. 210 km from its source, it joins the Alaknandā torrent going down from Nandā Devī in Devaprayāga—at an altitude of 7,800 m— becoming the Ganges river itself.

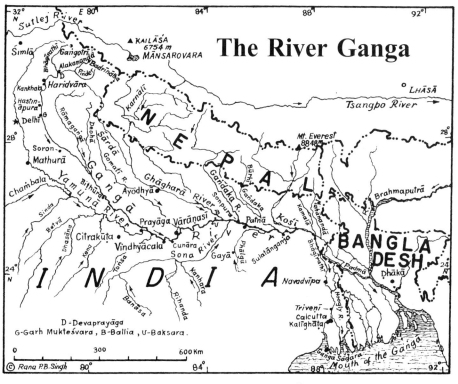

Then it flows from Haridwār, located at 300 m above sea level, through the Indian north plain, called the Ganges plain, becoming more even, flowing slowly while gathering a number of tributaries such as the Yamunā (1 300 km), the Ghaghrā (1080 km) in Chāpra, the Gandak (700 km) in Hajipur, the Rāmgangā (640 km) just before reaching Allāhābād, the Son (784 km) in Patna, the Dāmodarā— or Dāmodar- (541 km) in the south of Kolkata, the Koshī (700 km) close to Bhagalpur, the Gumtī—or Gomatī—(675 km) near Vārānasī…It flows into the Bay of the Bengal by forming an important delta called Sundarbans, where it joins with the Brahmaputra. A branch of this delta forms the Hūglī, which feeds Kolkata; the other major branch that flows into Bangladesh receives the name of Padmā before joining the Brahmaputra.

"Gaṅgā Mātā ki Jai!" Victory to Ma Gaṅgā.

Victory to Gaṅgā! Victory to Shiva!
O Gaṅgā, born of the urn of Brahmā
You who descended from the hair of Shiva
To wash away the sense of all men,
Purify them and increase their happiness!
You are the sustained of all living creatures here below!
I think of you and I bathe in your waters.
Consent to erase my sins and deliver me from evil.

The bodies, among others, of holy men and women (sādhus sādhvi), as well as young children, pregnant women, those dying of snake bites or smallpox (etc)—considered to be already pure—are not burnt: they are wrapped in a white linen and immersed into the holy water of the Ganges.

The Hindus regard the Ganges as a holy river. In Kāshī, the Ganges has yet to flow for another 1300 km before it reaches the sea. The immersion in the Ganges is supposed to wash the believer's sins away and the dispersal of ashes in the river can bring a better future life and even allows one to achieve moksha earlier, i.e. the release from the Samsāra, the cycle of reincarnation.

The Hindu devotees make pilgrimages to bathe in its water and meditate on its banks. Several Hindu holy sites are located along the banks of the Ganges, like Rishikesh, Haridwār (or Hardwār), Allahabad (Prayāga) and Vārānasī (Kāshī or Banāras).

In spite of the pollution, previously noticed by the American writer Mark Twain during his journey to the town of Vārānasī, in the 19th century, the Ganges is still a rich and special ecosystem: there are two species of dolphins, the Ganges dolphin (or Platanista Gangestica) and the Irrawaddy dolphin or Orcaella brevirostris, as well as an Indian crocodile Gavialis gangeticus, the Indian gharial and at the delta Glyphis gangeticus or Ganges shark.

It is estimated that each day the Ganges receives the remains of some 400 human corpses as well as the 1,550 tons of wood used for the cremations, to which the 9,000 carcasses of animals, which are abandoned there, have to be added. All of this is an important pollution factor. Various methods were planned to help clean it, such as the installation of purification stations and a system of hundreds of kilometres of sewers linking them, the construction of thousands of public toilets and electric crematoriums, as those found in Vārānasī, but they are hardly used but by the indigent population. Thousands of ghoul tortoises were released into the river so that they would eat the insufficiently burnt corpses, however, these animals were caught and eaten by the poor local residents.

However, the Ganges has an astonishing capacity of self-cleaning. It enjoys an oxygenation ten to twenty times higher than any other river in the world. It thus eliminates, thanks to its bacteria, some 80 % of the organic pollution every 2 km -covered in 30 minutes. However, its natural capacities are fast becoming insufficient today especially in the lower reaches near the large industrial towns that have developed along her banks.

Each year, the monsoon raises the level of the waters by several meters, affecting everybody's regular habits. But sometimes these increases are much more significant than envisaged, and in 1948, 1978 and 1982 the river water overflowed its banks, reaching 73.5 m (the danger level being recognised as 71.3 m).

The Hindus call it "Mother", "Ma Gangā", venerate it, adore it, give it all kinds of offerings and build huge temples in its honour on its consecrated land.

THE HOLY WATER

"You, fortifying Water, give us strength, greatness, Joy, vision

…Greatest of all wonders, ruler of people, the Water.

…You Water, make healing complete so that my body may be protected and I will see the sun for a long time to come…

…You, Water, wash away whatever sin I have committed, whatever wrong I have done to anyone, the perjury of which I have been guilty."

THE GODDESS GANGĀ

Gangā is the goddess of the Ganges. She is Shiva's wife, who bears her in his hair. She is sometimes called Bhagīrathī, "Bhagīratha's descendant".

According to the legend, Brahmā collected the sweat from the feet of Vishnu to create the Ganges thus blessed twice through the contact with two gods. A few years later, the king of Ayodhyā, an ancestor of Rāma called Sagar had by magic sixty thousand children. Sagar practised 100 times the Ashvamedha or the Horse Sacrifice. At the time of the last sacrifice the jealous god Indra stole the sacrificial horse and hid it in the wise but fierce sage Kapila Muni's āshram. As he could not find the horse, Sagar sent all his children to look for it. They found it at Kapila Muni's āshram and accused him of

ghosts wandered around the earth because their funerary rites had not been carried out.

When Bhagīratha, one of the Sagar's descendants, from a second wife, found out about his ancestors' fate, he made the wish to bring the Ganges down to the Earth in order to sweep the ashes of Sagar's children towards the sky. Bhagīratha asked Brahmā, who granted him his request and ordered Gangā to comply. Gangā, full of vanity, reckoned that she had been insulted and decided to sweep the whole Earth away.

Alarmed, Bhagīratha urged Shiva to break the strength of the torrential flood of the Ganges who fell with arrogance on the head of Shiva. But the god imprisoned her in his hair, gave her the epithet of Gangādhara and she emerged subdued and three times blessed through her contact with the whole Trimūrti.

The vehicle of the goddess Gangā is either a species of crocodile, the Indian Gharial (Gavialis Gangeticus), or a aquatic creature, know as the Makara.

Gangā receives a certain number of epithets: Armantyanādi, Mandākinī, Tripathaga, Bhagīrathī, Kirāti, Devabhutī, Khāpagā, Harashekarā (Shiva's crest), Mahābhadrā…The term Gangā itself is used to describe all the Indian rivers which are regarded as sacred.

being a thief. Then, the wise man opened his eyes for the first time in many years, stared at the sixty thousand children of Sagar and turned them into ashes, and their

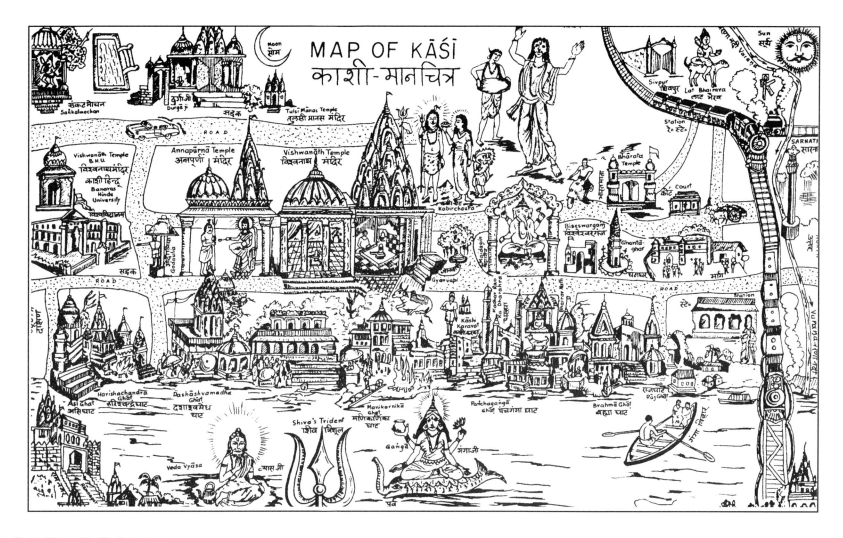

Map of Kāśī / काशी-मानचित्र

COSMOGONY
(mythical account of the formation of the universe)

The Hindu religion holds that human order was brought into being at the creation of the world. 'Therefore, cosmosisation of a territory of habitat is always a consecration and represents the paradigmatic works of gods' (Rana P B Singh in Cultural and Spiritual Guide of the Varanasi Region). The structure of the city is thus directly linked with these beliefs. It is conceived like a mandala and bears in itself all the elements of the Creation.

There are three different levels to understand Kāśhī: micro, meso and macro cosmos. Five is the number of Shiva and comprises a concept of totality, plenitude, global scope, and universality. Five is also the number of the five elements; the sky, the earth, the air (or ether), the water and the fire. This number is of capital importance in the Hindu symbolic system. According to a popular legend the five Tīrtha (holy places), called Panchatīrthī - where each pilgrim must take a bath—represent five body

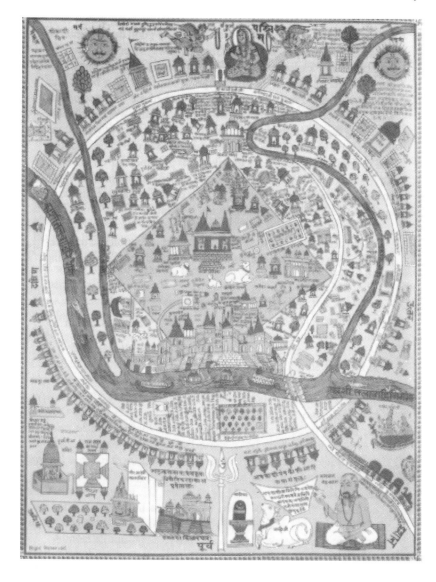

parts of God: Asi is the head, Dashāshvamedha is the chest, Manikarnikā is the navel, Panchagangā represents the thighs, and Ādi Keshava would be the feet. There are

five sacred roads in Kāshī, five ways of pilgrimage (Chaurashikroshī, Panchakroshī, Nagar Pradakshinā, Avimukta, Antargriha). Their layout has a precise significance. The city itself is built according to this plan. The temples are located according to this layout. The city is regarded as a body, a being, Kāshī the eternal breath. One reaches, through this cosmogony (this concept of the universe and man) a specific and intimate bond between the humane and the divine. The presence of Shiva reveals itself through the five senses (hearing, sight, touch, smell, taste), but also through the five elements. The holy mantra in the honour of Shiva "Na-Mah-Shi-Vā-Ya" has five syllables and five words and represents the unity between the man (humanity) and the cosmos (divinities).

According to the Ancients, the structure of the creation is based upon three stages: the evolution, the existence, and the eternal cyclical process. The Hindu Pantheon comprises the three most important gods: Brahmā, the Creator, Vishnu the Protector, the Preserver, and Shiva the Destroyer. In the Hindu cosmogony, Kāshī is believed to stand on Shiva's trident. Kāshī is at the crossroads where the humane and the divine meet. This explains the strength of the spiritual attractiveness of the city. And so Hindus say of Banāras that it stands at the centre of the earth as the place of creation, and gathers together the whole of the sacred universe in a single symbolic circle, a mandala. Yet, it is not an earthly city. Kāshī is said to sit above the earth as a "crossing place" (thīrtha) between this world and the "far shore" of the transcendent Brahman (Diana L. Eck: Banāras city of light).

ONE DAY IN KĀSHĪ

ONE DAY IN KĀSHĪ

The sun has not yet risen. Everywhere small bells tinkle accompanied by the long call to prayer from a remote muezzin. These Oriental recitative chants, and the metal sound of the small bells produce a strange and spellbinding atmosphere. The relentless striking of the dhobīs (washermen) already washing the linen marks the rhythm of the early morning yet to arrive. A morning mist wraps the banks of the Ganges with its vaporous coat. All the contours and the relief are softened by a delicate fog, which gives a feeling of melancholy. Cotton-like-wrapped, the palaces are covered with a mysterious air. Kāshī slowly wakes up.

Nonchalantly, the small boats glide over the water. As smooth as a mirror, the Ganges flows unrelentingly. Here we find a feeling of eternity that nothing, nor no one, could disturb except the occasional jump of a dolphin.

The small bells ring. A sādhu rhythmicaly recites his mantras along the river. In this half lit atmosphere, running towards the places of devotion, silhouettes move taking short steps. The incense burns and pervades the whole city just like the acrid fumes of the Manikarnikā pyres that last all night long and have been active for Millenniums. Manikarnikā has never stopped reducing the dead bodies to ashes.

On the bank, scabies ridden starving dogs sleep intertwined on still hot ashes. In the distance, a patchwork sail glides slowly and majestically over the river, gentle in its approach. The golden reflections begin to dance on the waves. The small boats, slowly, perform a dance, which will not cease its whirling throughout the day. The incense sticks send their musky perfumes towards the sky.

As every morning, on a platform, which juts out into the main flow of the river, a pūjārī wearing a white and red dhoti officiates by himself in front of the rising star. The rising of the sun and the ceremonies that go with this event are privileged moments. The priest offers the sun a flame, as a symbol of life and purity. The swinging of this large oil lamp marks the arrival of the day and the eternity of life, the victory of the day over the night, of the light over the darkness. This mystical dance celebrates the gods and the life. It is a message of hope. Behind him, a woman strikes hard on a bell, which tinkles at the top of its voice. The man blows into his conch producing long piercing sounds. He sends messages to the gods only they can decipher. He draws himself up, sending streams of fire towards the sky. Majestic and fluid in its mystical choreography facing the Ganges, he serenely turns to the four cardinal points. He offers a sacred dance to the world and the gods. His fire cobra dances in the air. This moment is always magic, because it takes place in the intimacy of the early morning. It is like an invitation to life, to the coming day.

A light hot wind starts to blow. The ghāts are still calm. A few groups of barefoot pilgrims get dressed. There is a friendly atmosphere. Some have their heads shaved by skilful barbers, while the ghātiās are already at work under their parasols. The grandmothers meticulously prepare their offerings: flowers, burning earthen lamps (dīpa), leaves, magic cure-all powders…The mothers make the most of it and clean their reluctant children. The soap foams on their faces, and stings the still sleepy eyes. On the steps, others rub their teeth vigorously with a maragosa (neem) stick. Some women sprinkling apply them selves lots of water and one feels that this moment does not only have a religious connotation, but it is also a social act. It is the moment of the day when women meet up to chat. Laughter is heard. The children play about in the water. The prayers mingle with the children's shouts, and my mind, this morning, lets itself daydream freely.

And then there is this woman I had observed on several occasions. She is there, full of dignity, upright, and her hands held together, in deep meditation. And if you look carefully, you can see tears running down her face. In silence, facing the rising sun, she points her sorrows towards the skies. Her eyes show the pain. I vanish.

I stroll about on the ghāts and let myself be imbued by this atmosphere of meditation and life explosion. To one side, a man reads the newspaper, turned towards the river. Any good news? Wedged in the cracks of the thousand-years-old stones, the air slowly softens— aromatised by incense sticks. Further away, a woman, dressed completely in white—a widow—deposits leaves dedicated to the worship of Shiva (bael patra) on the marble. With her finger, twisted by age, she marks five small red lines for each of the five elements (sky, earth, air, water, fire). She lights a small bowl of fire, which she whirls in the air. Then, she spins round on herself three times; one turn for Shiva, one for Vishnu and, finally, one for Brahmā. That is the āratī, brief moments of mystical brightness. Inscriptions cover the steps. It could be easily taken for prayers or mantras. There are just the names of those who saw their carnal shroud flying away in smoke in Manikarnikā and whose families have wished to favour their karma by offering the Ganges these immaculate steps. These ancient rituals are like the Ganges itself, with its eternal course, the image of a perpetual motion that nothing can stop.

A little further, Anup repairs one of his small boats. Slowly the city wakes up, and everyone starts their activities again, relieved by the purification of the waters. Alleviated by the conversation they have held with the gods, time can again take its normal course. The life here is absolutely unique, not only because of the devotions practised here by everyone, but also because it is life itself that is here, in its pure state, with its goodness and its hardship. Life itself mixes up with death in a spellbinding melancholy litany. There are families, their children twirling around their kites, defying weightlessness. In the distance, smoke columns indicate the cremation sites: Manikarnikā ghāt, Harischandra ghāt. One sādhu, after his ritual ablutions, coats his naked body with ashes collected from the pyres. Dust you are, dust you shall become again…A man shaves the head of another man, fully dressed in white, the colour of bereavement. He only leaves him a little black tuft of hair hanging on top of his scalp. He will most probably go to ignite the pyre of a close relative, surely his father…The elder son of the departed must go five times round the pyre, with a torch in his hand before putting fire to it starting at the head. These five convolutions recall the five elements. A huge wooden heap waits there for the moment to consume the corpse with its flames, hundreds of such bodies arrive in the city every day. Provided with large bamboos, sweat-soaked men knock on the logs and the carbonised bodies that seem to resist to the oblivion and do not want to bend. Feet are sticking out of the flames. Blackened limbs stick out, like a last hope. On the side, bodies lying down on a bamboo stretcher await their turn in front of the Ganges. Children and gold-washers try to recover jewels, gold teeth or other valuable items, that they will tear off the dead. The Dom's family is in charge of providing the necessary holy fire for all the cremations. This fire, supervised day and night for millenniums, never died out. Invasions, monsoons, nothing has ever stopped it. This fire is like the Ganges: eternal....At that point, the sun is a ball of reddish and imposing fire in the still grey sky.

Further away, a veiled Muslim woman, totally dressed in black, shows only one rectangle of life. She embarks on a barge in the company of her husband and her child whom she tightly holds in her arms—in so doing, seeking to reassure him, to reassure herself.

On returning to Dashāshvamedh, the women let their bright coloured sarīs slip on the steps, they only wear one light blouse and a cotton underskirt. They descend the three steps leading to the purifying river, sprinkling holy water onto themselves whilst reciting healing mantras. A copper bowl in hand: a "tāmar lota", copper pots used to get the water from the Ganges. They stretch their arms, then they fold them back to the chest, they present the sun with this purifying water, slowly pouring its content. They seem to put their destiny, their very humanity into the flow of the nourishing river. They recite, they chant, and then submerge themselves three consecutive times till their whole selves are completely clean and purified in the stream. Then they return to the bank and offer the Ganges tiny trays of scintillating flowers. They cast orange and red petals on the steps.

Men carry out their devotions calmly, covered simply with a single cloth. Sometimes, on their shoulders and along their side, a cord (Janeū) marks their status as being of the second born. All of them celebrate the approaching day as if it were a gift the gods, a godsend from the Earth. However, it has not always showed gratitude to them, and suffices to read in their eyes to perceive the mysteries, to catch a glimpse of the hardship of existence, the challenge of life. There are separate ghāts for women and for men. Multicoloured sarīs are mixed together, hustled and immersed. There is a mixture of holiness and familiarity, an alchemy of routines. Religion is in easy reach of the faithful Hindus. It is more than a religion or a philosophy of life, it is itself an integral aspect of life. It is the life and its raison to be. The gods and the Ganges are like flesh and blood entities one gets close to with the greatest intimacy, in an unreasoned and irrational respect. The whole of Kāshī is a prayer.

To the side, an old slim sādhu, removes his orange robes in order to practise his ablutions. Dressed in a simple loincloth, hunchbacked, he advances towards the holy water with slow steps. He undoes his dreadlock hair (that falls to his knees) and squats on the stone. He takes the liquid to his mouth, does his ablutions and then comes back, trembling, gracefully. He grabs his hair together and rolls it up on itself to make a bulky, perfect bun.

A huge number of ghāts stretch along the banks of the river, exactly eighty-four. Some have deep colours—like the heart of the city—others have softer colours. A man leads his buffaloes to the water with the intention of bathing them. The spectacle of these enormous animals descending the steps skilfully is highly impressive. The buffaloes seem at ease in the water whereas on the side, cows bask in the sun. The dhobīs wash the clothes by carelessly beating them on the immersed stones. Women collect cow dung to make quite useful cakes later used to fuel their ovens when they are dried. A hairdresser trims the moustache of a customer. Children play, free from care.

From the top of the Nepali temple, the view overlooks the river. With the shape of a pagoda, sustained by carved wood pillars where scenes of the Kāmasūtra are found, this temple is a haven of peace. Old women chat at the entrance. Some monkeys jump from one branch to another before clutching themselves to the surrounding wall. A splendid and winding pīpal tree (ficus religiosa) has snatched paper kites from the children. Here in Kāshī, this is the favourite kids' game, but the adults are also fond of it. And whether it is from the terraces, balconies or from the banks of the Ganges, tens of multicoloured kites fly into the azure sky.

The sun sends its rays onto the old palaces and the ancestral residences, all of them of a delicate and imposing style. It illuminates the buildings with a soft and profound light. Even the slightest relief gives shape to the construction, providing it with a breath of life. In front of an old palace with blood-red walls, a trident planted in the ground indicates the presence of a sādhu. He chats with two friends. Sitting on a headland, a group of women intonate bewitching songs, the so-called bhajans. All the banks are crowded with small groups of devotees that splash with one another and dive. Some soap or shampoo themselves, other do their washing up or clean their clothes. Further away, a group of fishermen tidy up and repair their nets. On the side, a kid covers a section of the wall with cow dung cakes to dry them.

The rays of the sun have become frightening weapons. They flatten the city with their might, now completely awake. Four girls paint the palaces along the Ganges using watercolours. Committed to their craft, the sketches emerge a little by little. Colours are spread over the canvas and a whole world of mystery comes to life. Further on, the dhobīs (washermen) beat the clothes with full force against the stones lying next to the water. There are many of them, men and women. On the bank, and on the large wall that overhangs it (there is not a single gap left), shirts, trousers, white sheets and other multicoloured sarīs cover the ground everywhere like colourful garlands. A little further away, a cow, decorated with garlands of flowers, draws our attention. It is a ceremony of the cow, a cow pūjā (Gao dhan). Humming strange mantras, the participants throw some flowers onto the back of the animal, and then some drops of holy water. They spin on themselves clockwise, hands together, bowing in front of the animal. The veneration of the cow is not a vane issue in Kāshī. Good natured, and with the appearance of not understanding a thing the animal lets them carry on.

On Mīr ghāt, children play joyfully in the water. A diving contest is organized. Carefree, they play, start to dance yelling their joy, waving their arms towards the sky. On the heights, a terrace is used as a gym by some wrestlers. This is an akhārā. A man swings an Indian club (a bamboo stick attached to a large weight called a gada) behind his back from side to side. Relentlessly, he keeps this swinging, like a clock in perpetual motion. Some children play cricket, while others watch them in front of a palace. Defeated by the heat, a man sleeps on the chowki (wooden bench) of a ghātiā, with a child's windmill in his hand. Further on, a travelling musician is having a nap, his head resting on his harmonium. Only the children and the animals put up with the heat. On the branches of a tree, two parrots sqawk, under the curious glance of a monkey. I have never been to a city with so many different species of animals: monkeys, cows, bulls, dogs, parrots, ducks, geese, buffaloes, dolphins, swallows, eagles, squirrels, donkeys, mules, horses, lizards mosquitoes, butterflies, goats, cocks, hens,

cats…This entire mini world lives here in freedom and perfect harmony.

A few metres away, we find the little Ravi with his naked torso, proud under the bright sun. He is a small-time salesman, a street kid. Ravi is only nine years old, but has the silhouette, the gawky look and the self-confidence of a small man. It is necessary to grow quickly in Kāshī when one has to pull through life. Relentlessly, he throws an object tied up to a string, which he brings back as if he had fished something. What may be the fruit of his miraculous fishing? He shows me a magnet called "chumbak" attached at the end of the rope and a coin- stuck to it. He has already fished thirty rupees this morning.

Overwhelmed by the incipient heat, the Chausatthī ghāt with its geometrical shapes lead directly to the lanes. It is cool there; the half-light favours an atmosphere of meditation and serenity. The statues of altars nestling in a hundred-years-old pīpal tree seem to have witnessed the passing of thousands of generations of pilgrims. Some have suffered the ravages of time, and their silhouettes have shaded off under the touches of the believers. Having arrived at the temple of Chausatthī, a slender man repaints its walls in a relaxing blue, as found everywhere in Kāshī, especially in the temples. People enter and leave once they have bowed over, prayed, quickly bowing to the gods and their souls. After whispering some prayers and bowing, they proceed again with their daily activities, assured with divine protection.

A well is installed in the entrance. Old women come to stock up by painfully pumping at the handpump. The painter comes down from his bamboo ladder. The sound of a sitar comes from a small dark room. The possibilities and the variations that this instrument offers are innumerable. The priest of the temple makes his fingers slide across the sitar neck. The twists and turns of these sonorities lead my mind to nomad worlds, to a different time in history. I leave this place enraptured with the Orient.

A brass band passes along. It is a funeral procession. On a bamboo stretcher, the corpse swings to the rhythm of the bearers and the musicians. They chant: "Rāma nāma satya hai! Rāma nāma satya hai!" (The name of God is the Truth). The group of ten people quickly descends the alley towards Harischandra ghāt, carrying the dead towards the ultimate release "Kāshyām maranam muktih": (death in Kāshī is Liberation).

I wander up and down, strolling along the lanes, which appear to protect me from its ancestral walls. This is Chauk, the old city. The carved wooden doors, several centuries old, open onto tiny courtyards. The craggy and deep faces of the women around us, takes you, simultaneously, into a world of beauty and hardship.

Suddenly, a cow steps out galloping. In its race, it nervously raises its hind legs. Where does it go? To an urgent meeting? It is better to make way for the cow. But there is not enough room here. The alleys are so narrow that two widths of shoulders can barely cross. While passing in front of a dark alcove, a tiny bulb struggles to illuminate properly and where it is hardly possible to stand up, one can spot a great weaving loom. A crossed-leg man works. His young son besides him looks with suspicion—he seems to protect his father. The weaver, imperturbable, threads time and again his golden strings

in one direction, then in another for the glory and the very high reputation of the silk trade of Banāras. The silk cloth of Kāshī is regarded as one of the most beautiful in the world.

Shops and tiny booths mark out the lanes. There is a bit of everything to be bought in them: clothing, vegetables, flasks which will allow the pilgrims to bring back a little bit of holy water from the Ganges, local crafts, flowers, items to be used in several rituals...It is difficult to enumerate the whole gamut of goods. It is easy to notice it that the tradesmen gather together. Fruit vendors among fruit vendors, spice vendors among spice vendors, etc., and often it is the aroma that leads the way…

In one lane we find a whole variety of fresh milk products (cream cheese, condensed milk cakes and yoghurt (or curd) and sometimes fresh unsalted butter cubes). Here the men lean against the wall with the various products placed in front of them. The bargaining is very lively. Some gesticulate, others hail…On the other side, within two meters at the most, a few workshops form a line in raised recesses, in which two, three or four men sit. In the centre of the workshop an immense set of scales sits imposingly whose counterweights are made of heavy cast iron blocks.

The catering corner is a little further away. These stalls are called dhabas. On incandescent embers, large pastries are sizzling in enormous pans filled with bubbling oil. It looks very appetising, and here the Banārsīs, who eat standing up, are hardly misled: samosa, jalebī, pakorā, parāthā, all of that will be sold in tiny leave plates.

On a street corner, one finds the pān-walla (betel leaf seller). Around it, men speak with their mouth full of pān. It is not possible to understand much of what they say, but that does not bother them at all. Patiently, the pān-walla adds areca nuts and some spices to a pān leaf garnishing the chew. It is a tradition throughout India but especially in Kāshī, where it has an excellent reputation. Wherever you go, this red liquid can be seen in lanes and on walls.

Moving on, the lanes become busier once you reach the main road and leave Chauk. It is almost impossible to go forward, the traffic is so intense. No cars—they are banned in this area—but rickshaws, two wheelers and crowds everywhere. Cows in the middle of the crossroads bask quietly, ignoring the frenzy around them. There is no pavement. During the power failures, the generators release nauseous black fumes, as well as a hellish racket, even covering up the echo that comes out from the booming speakers. All is muddled in noisy anarchy: passers by and rickshaws, cows and mules, dogs and bulls, etc. When one reaches the crossroads of Godauliā, anarchy reaches its peak. On his central pedestal, a police officer threatens with his stick and tries to put order in the chaotic atmosphere, but to no avail. The bells of the rickshaws tinkle at the top of their voice while the horns of motorcycles sound their deadly howl. A demonstration passes by. Megaphones at the front, banners and flags follow the peaceful procession. That does not affect in the slightest the cows, who serenely, carry on their way, or decide to stop in the middle of the main crossroads. A man perched on a splendid black horse talks in the midst of the mayhem. His mount does not seem be bothered by the infernal traffic. This whole world raises a dust as if it was a desert storm, and the air becomes almost un-breathable. Sitting on the bare ground, a dentist treats a lady and extracts her teeth using pliers. He has beautiful blue eyes and bears proudly his pepper-and-salt dreadlocks that fall down to the bottom of his back. He has all his implements in front of him, some dentures and some moulds, used as prints.

The heat and the noise bring you back—as the obvious choice—towards the lanes of the Chauk. There are children enjoying an ice cream, girls who, from the top of a terrace, stare at the comings and goings below them. Then I walk further on, attracted by the clamours of a wedding. Drummers beat with frenzy the rhythm of a primitive trance. Children cling onto the windows to get a better view of the scene, while others dance with their arms raised towards the sky, like an offering, namely themselves. The bracelets around wrists and ankles tinkle with each swing of the body. Sweating women spin to the rhythm of the frantic beats, raised arms, swaying their body with an infinite grace in the Oriental way, majestically. They dance around. The young men take part in this dance in a state of ecstasy with an astonishing smoothness and fluidity. Beads of sweat shine on their foreheads, then all over their bodies. The hypnotic drumming takes over everybody's consciousness. And this small cosmos enters a transcendental mystical state. These are only the wedding preliminary stages. In the cement-floored house a goat is blocking the entrance, the rooms are dark and tiny. Women sit on the bare ground. Others pass around plates full of pastry dishes. Outside, a brass band waits for the moment when they shall play their trumpets and tubas. The colours of their uniforms are very bright. Then comes the moment to play the instruments to the rhythm of the big drums. The grandmothers appear, the men spit their pān. The ceremony of henna (mehandi) has already taken place and the drawings lined on the hands seem to be an initiatory code and the married couples shall be the bearers from now onwards. The festival has begun.

Slowly the day dies out. A seller of multicoloured candy-floss walks along the ghāts looking for a last customer. A sādhu watches the river. The afternoon is over. The last sunrays signal the beginning of the pūjā everywhere in the city. As to conjure away the bad luck the night could bring, everyone gathers to pray. In Dashāshvamedh the ceremonies start. Five promontories are placed. A gilded carpet covers them. On each one of them, a pūjārī officiates in a perfectly ordered dance. The same movements, the same ancestral gestures as a last offering to the setting sun, to the day as it comes to an end. During the whole ceremony, uncountable small bells jingle in the night, carrying with them divine spells. With light and perfectly synchronized hand movements, the pūjārī impregnate the air with an intoxicating incense aroma. Odorous clouds fly away towards the skies. Then, in the sparkling night, there they are, performing a perfect choreography as they make the flames dance in the direction of the four cardinal points.

A long call to the gods breaks the silence when priests blow to their conches. Have the gods heard this call? They start singing in the honour of Shiva, Pārvatī, Rāma…The gathering shouts: "Jai" (honour to you, respect) while raising their hands towards the vault of heaven, which from now on shall cover the city. Slowly, the priests move towards the Ganges to pour the water of the river they have had with them over this immutable ceremony. They are followed by the whole crowd, throwing petals and small bowls of flowers with a dancing flame in the middle onto the black water. They will descend the Ma Gangā.

The priests climb back to give out sweets to the devotees. These sweets are called prasād. It is time to return. Still late into the night, some bells ring out in the city as a call that the faithful give to the gods, who sometimes forget to deal with the humans. On the calm river, still some flowing boats glide along, lingering small golden lights in their trails. Slowly, under the stars that twinkle in the sky, Kāshī falls asleep.

"I imagine the mountains and the forests flying across the ages, I imagine that from the night the light shall come to life again at the encounter with every star…"

Rabindranath Tagore.

1

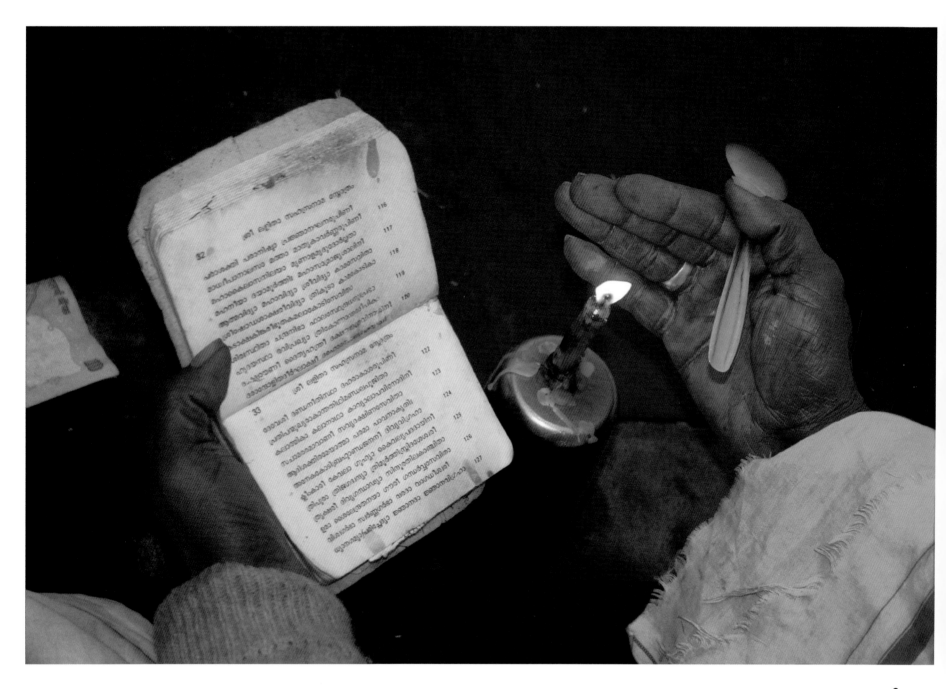

2

3

4

5

6 a, b, c

40

7

8

9

10

11

13

14

15

17

18

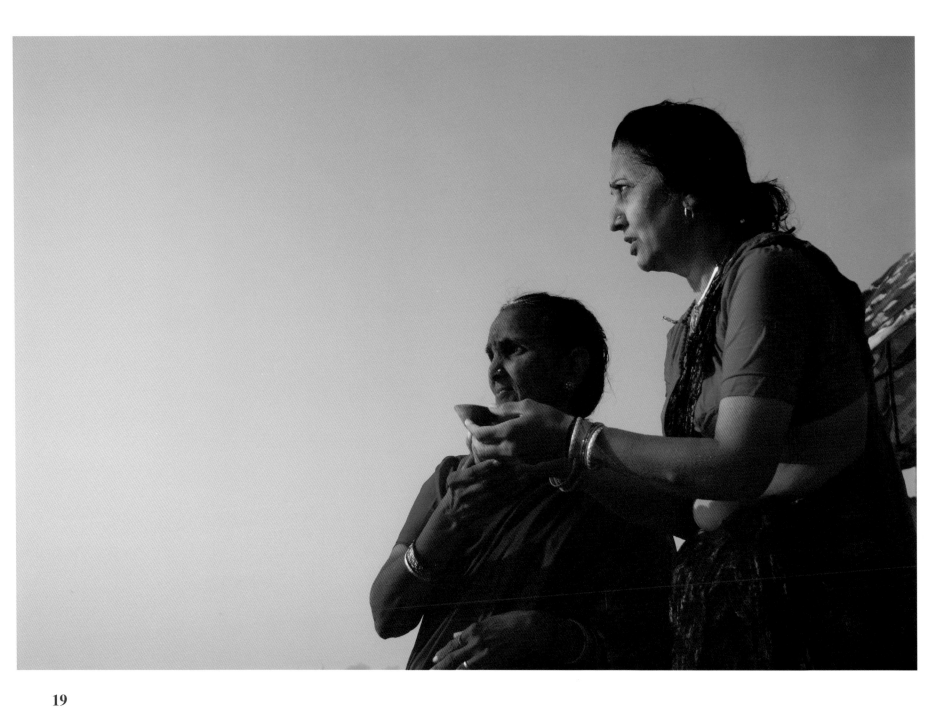

19

20

21

23 a, b, c, d

57

25

27 a, b

28 a, b, c

29 a, b

33

35

36 a, b, c

37

38

39

41

43

45

46

47

48

49

51

53 a, b, c

55

56

59 a, b, c

61

63

64 a, b

65

67

68

69

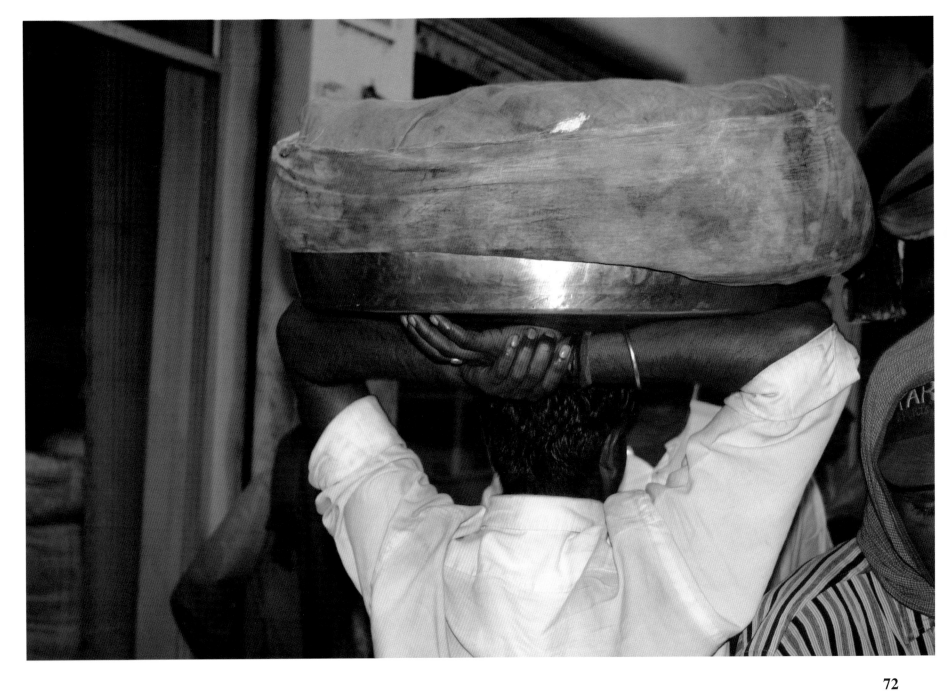

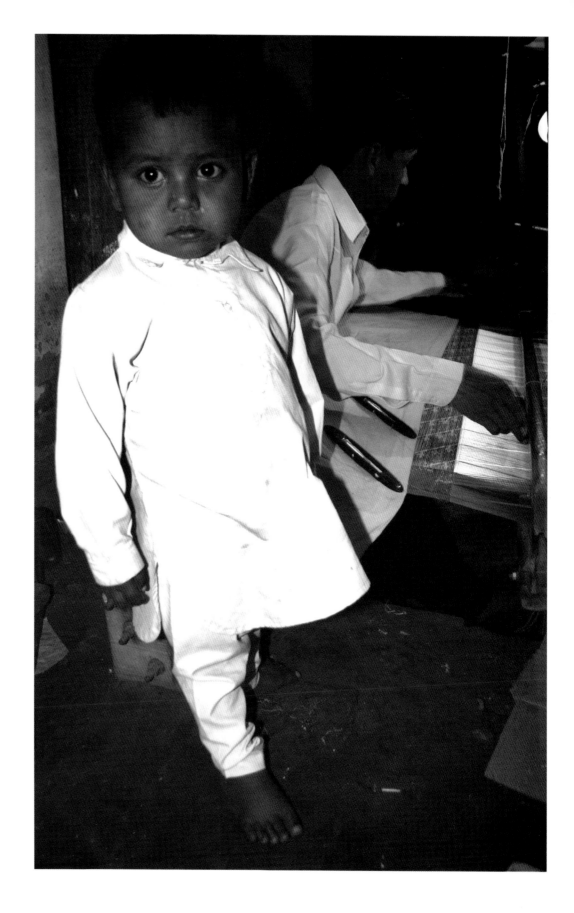

73

75

77

78

79

80

81

82 a, b

83

84

118

85

87

89

91

93

94

95 a, b, c, d

97

98

99

102

103

105 a, b, c

107

1. Sādhu (holy man) in the fog: Mīr ghāt
2. Sādhu (holy man) reciting mantras and other prayers Mīr ghāt
3. Boatman in the rising sun
4. Morning pūjā, at the sunrise
5. Boat on Gangā with the rising sun.
6. a) Morning pūjā, during sunrise. This ritual instrument is a Kapūrdānī. The pūjārī is calling the gods. He tries to awake them with the flame. The cobra is used to cover the fire in the event of rain. The cobra represents Shiva and Vishnu b) Morning pūjā with the censer called Dhūpdānī filled with sandal powder, cow dung on coal. Incense is used to wake up the gods. The cloth worn by pūjārī, this kind of dhoti is called: Dupatta c) Morning puja during the sunrise. Kapūrdānī is the name of this ritual instrument. The pūjārī is calling the gods. He tries to awake them with the flame. The cobra is used to cover the fire in the event of rain. The cobra represents Shiva and Vishnu
7. Man in the fog. Digpatia ghāt
8. Pigeons flying away in the fog: Panchagangā ghāt
9. Three little dogs are heated on still hot ashes
10. Prayers during the rising sun for sun god called Surya
11. Women joining for the same flame to light the incense. The incense is used to awake the Gods.
12. Hibiscus flowers and rice in offering for the gods
13. This leaf with three branches ("Bael Patra") represents the trident of Shiva (trishūl). Rice is a gift for the gods. Red powder is called Kumkum. Devotees put five lines of vermilion powder to be lucky. It represents the five gross elements: sky, earth, air, water and fire. It's also a prayer for Ganesh.
14. A widow is praying with candle. Dashāshvamedh ghāt. Many widows come to Vārānasī waiting for the death. We know that she is a widow because she has no more red line on the hair. Married women in India are required to wear sindūr in the parting of their hair
15. With candles, kumkum (vermilion past) and sweets, a woman is praying to Gangā.
16. Jalashiyi ghāt, Khiraki ghāt and Manikarnikā ghāt. Faraway, we can see the flames of funeral pyres. Day and night, many cremations take place. More than 30,000 cremations take place here every year.
17. Rajendra Prasād ghāt and Dashāshvamedh ghāt. The body of a man, surmounted by two crows, is floating on the Gangā.
18. Woman praying with the Kamandal on the forehead.
19. Women praying with candles. After having turned with circular motions with the flame, they make three turns on themselves: one for Shiva, one for Vishnu and one for Brahmā.
20. Ahilyā bāī ghāt. Holy dip in the morning. This rite of purification is called Snān. To immerse itself in Gangā purifies the body and the heart. We can observe the ghātiās platform. Ghātiās are priests who officiate on the ghāt.
21. Ahilyā bāī ghāt. Holy dip in the morning. We can see pilgrims who fill some cans with water of Gangā.
22. A broken marble step at Dashāshvamedh ghāt
23. a) Woman praying on Prayāga ghāt. Steps are in marble stone. Inscriptions are names of dead people. Families have paid for these stones to help the dead to have Moksha. Moksha is the liberation of reincarnation cycle for going to heaven. b) Old woman (widow) with Kamandal in the hand. c) Old Woman taking holy dip for purification. (Snān). d) Old sādhu (holy man) going to Gangā for holy dip (Snān).
24. A woman is praying near Gangā on Dashāshvamedh ghāt, with a "tāmar lota" in her hand. This is a brass pot used to draw water of Gangā.
25. Young Brahmin having the Shikhā, little tuft of hair. He is making again the node that remembers the Brahmā hairdo.
26. Young girl going to take the ritual holy dip in Gangā, (Snān) for purification
27. a) Old woman. She is a widow because she has no more red line on the hair. Married women in India are required to wear sindūr in the parting of their hairs. She is going to take holy dip (Snān). She has a tank to fill of Gangā water. Dashāshvamedh ghāt b) Old sādhu (holy man), after taking ritual holy dip (Snān)
28. a) Young girl taking holy dip with water of Gangā. The name of the pot is "lota". Prayāga ghāt b) Young Brahmin praying. We know that he is Brahmin because he carries a cord named Janeū c) Little girl with doll on Prayāga ghāt
29. a) Old woman (widow) making pūjā with offerings, camphor lamps for the gods. Dashāshvamedh ghāt b) Old woman before holy dip on Dashāshvamedh ghāt
30. Two women making the washing by hands on the steps of marble. Prayāga ghāt. One is a widow (she is wearing a white sari, colour of bereavement).
31. Woman after taking ritual holy dip (Snān)
32. In the morning: woman on Gangā reading a prayer book
33. Sindūr (vermilion paste) marks for pūjā, with sweets and flowers on the steps. The red marks represent the five gross elements: sky, earth, air, water and fire
34. Camphor lamp, sandalwood, incense, flowers and sweets (prasād) for the pūjā on the steps

35. Lingam with mālā (garland of flowers). The lingam is the sign or emblem of Shiva and the focus of Shiva worship. There is a snake (Kundalini) on the lingam, which is the symbol of Shiva it represents the energy. Behind, we can see also a Nandī (a bull representing the vehicle of Shiva. It symbolizes justice and rightness)

36. a) Kamandal with water of Gangā and flowers for doing pūjā b) Nandī statue. Nandī (the bull) is the vehicle of Shiva. It symbolizes justice and rightness c) Two Shiva's lingam, (one in silver, the other in marble), incense pot, conch, flowers, mālā (necklace of flowers), statue of Ganesh on the ghāt for praying

37. Lingam with flowers and leaf of bael patra (which is leaf with three parts which symbolize the trinity Shiva, Vishnu, Brahmā). The lingam is the sign or emblem of Shiva and the focus of Shiva worship. There is a snake (Kundalini) on the lingam that is the symbol of Shiva it represents the energy

38. Women making pūjā, praying and singing (bhajans) ritual songs

39. There are offerings (prasād) for the gods: fruits, rice, and sweets

40. Women coming from Bihār for the Dālā Chath festival (month of Kārttik, November), doing pūjā, praying and singing (bhajans) ritual songs. There are offerings (prasād) to the gods: fruits, rice, sweets

41. Women coming from Bihār for the Dālā Chath festival (month of Kārttik, November), making pūjā, praying and singing (bhajans) ritual songs. There are offerings (prasād) for the gods: fruits, rice, sweets

42. Grand-mother (widow), mother and daughter coming from Bihār for the Dālā Chath festival (month of Kārttik, November).

43. Old sādhu (holy man) doing the ritual make-up of the face. Prayāga ghāt

44. a) Old man with pearl mālā (rosary with 108 beads) round his neck going to make pūjā on Gangā banks b) Sādhu (holy man) on the ghāt with the Vishnu tilak on his face c) Woman with Vishnu tilak on her forehead

45. Old sādhu (holy man) looking Gangā. Attributes of the Sādhu: Shiva's trident (trishūl), the three teeth represent Shiva, Brahmā and Vishnu, Shiva's drum called Damaru, mālā (rosary with 108 beads). He is carrying everything he has. Rāja ghāt

46. Sādhu looking at the Gangā

47. Ahilyā bāī ghāt, Sādhu sitting with a dog in front of Vishnu and Brahmā statue

48. Dog sitting in Munshi ghāt

49. Banks of Gangā, general view. We can see the beautiful blue house, which is the house of the Dom family. Dom Family who care the burning ghāts and the holy fire

50. Man reading the newspaper in Dashāshvamedh ghāt

51. Man who is selling flowers for offerings to Gangā on Prayāga ghāt

52. Mother Gangā temple in Lalitā ghāt. A man is making beauty hairstyle

53. a) Pilgrims coming from Mahārāshtra. Those women are drying saris on the steps of Rāja ghāt b) Women drying saris on the banks of Gangā c) Sarveshvara ghāt. Drying clothes

54. Women are taking cow dung to make dry cakes for fuel on Rāj ghāt. Cow dung is also sacred. Behind there is a red bridge named Mālavīya Bridge after the founder of Banāras Hindu University

55. From Rāma ghāt. Man being massaged in the morning. We can see the Alamgir mosque built in 1673 by the bigoted Mughal emperor Aurangzeb

56. Woman after holy dip with her children in Dashāshvamedh ghāt

57. Little boy in front of a Bhismpitāmah statue. Rāma ghāt

58. Barber and customer on Prayāga ghāt

59. a) Barber waiting for customers b) Man cutting his beard on the Gangā banks. Dashāshvamedh ghāt c) Barber shaving the head as purification for funeral ritual

60. Old woman with blue eyes. She is a widow because she is wearing a white sari, and she has no red mark on parting of her hair. Married women in India are required to wear sindūr in the parting of their hair. Rajendra Prasād ghāt

61. Pilgrim coming from Gujarāt in Panchagangā ghāt. She is married because she is wearing a silver necklace called mangal sutra

62. Before a festival, a man is making again the painting of Vishnu, which beautifies the water tank of Rajendra Prasād ghāt

63. Kedāra ghāt. Woman going to Gangā for holy dip

64. a) Nārada ghāt. Buffaloes. They are also used for milk b) Boy on a buffalo at Nārada ghāt

65. Man selling candyfloss on the banks. Rāja ghāt

66. Indian time "A clock without hands", Lakshmī and Ganesh statue

67. An old woman contemplating the Gangā

68. Harmonium player sleeping on his instrument on Dashāshvamedh ghāt. He is an itinerant musician, coming from Bengal

69. Man sleeping on ghātiā place in Prayāga ghāt

70. Man sleeping in front of his shop of paper bags. Shivālā road

71. Boy and girl eating an ice cream in the street of the Chauk

72. Man carrying freshly made cottage cheese at Chauk

73. Child with his father making silk saris at Chauk. Kāshī is a city very famous all over the world for the silk production, saris and brocades

74. Chaussathī ghāt stairs under the sun

75. Wrestler after exercise in the Akharā at Badahar Kothī

76. Krishna temple near the flower market

77. A cow inside the house and a woman at Chauk

78. Woman carrying a basket on her head at Chauk

79. A cobbler smoking a bīdī (Indian cigarettes) and a boy in Bengāli Tolā

80. Old woman. Portrait

81. Man with a turban and red beard on Dashāshvamedh ghat

82. a) Old man with turban b) Man with turban. We can see on his lips red mark of pān (betel). This is a thousand-year-old chewing habit a very common habit in Vārānasī. It relieves hunger, stimulates the organs of digestion, and disinfects the breath. Banarasi leaves are the most favoured

83. Ceremony: cow pūjā in Dashāshvamedh ghat. The Cow is considered to be a goddess. The woman is making the cow wet with water of Gangā

84. Mān Singh Palace with children looking Gangā. Mān Mandir ghat: this ghat and this palace were built by the Mahārāja of Jaipur Savai Mān Singh in 1600. At the top of the palace there is an observatory built in 1710 by Savai Jai Singh II

85. Very holy and sacred fire of the burning ghat of Manikarnikā. Night and day, this fire is kept by the Dom family since millenniums and has never died. The guard of the holy fire is bowing down before the flames. We can see two Shiva's tridents, (trishūl), and a heap of wood for cremations

86. Men are praying in the Mahā Mrityuanjai temple. Their right hand is hidden in a glove for using the rosary (Mālā). The prayer is an intimate act

87. Women in Hanumān Temple (Sankat Mochan Mandir)

88. Man whitewashing inside Chausatthī temple, near Chausatthī ghat

89. Reflection in water. Manikarnikā ghat. Women doing pilgrimage in Kāshī are carrying big bags on the head

90. Near Lalitā ghat, women doing a pilgrimage in Kāshī are carrying big bags on the head

91. Impression of Vishnu's feet: Cārana Pāduka in Manikarnikā ghat. Through the centuries millions of Hindus have wetted it with the holy Gangā water and adorned it with flowers. It is considered as the holiest place in the sacred City

92. Mīr ghat little boy jumping in Gangā

93. Mīr ghat children dancing after swimming in Gangā

94. With the grandmother

95. a) Husband and wife after marriage b) Hand of the husband with henna before the wedding c) Hands with henna during wedding ceremony. At home d) Husband and wife painting their hands with henna during the wedding ceremony in Prayāga ghat

96. Woman dancing to the drum beat during a wedding

97. Three women dancing to the drum beat during a wedding

98. Child with poster of a Bollywood studio actress and a poster of Shiva and Pārvatī in his room

99. Beautiful tree in Nepali temple near Gangā. Lalitā ghat

100. Sādhu (holy man) walking on the banks with a rosary (mālā) and big turban to put his very long dreadlocks, more than two metres. Rāja ghat

101. Beautiful married woman going to pray in the Durgā temple. She has the red mark of sindūr her forehead: mark of the married woman. Married women in India are required to wear sindūr in the parting of their hair

102. Young woman is praying on the smoke during the festival of Dālā Chath (November, month of Kārttik)

103. Women are lighting the 108 flames for the night pūjā. Dashāshvamedh ghat

104. Night pūjā in front of Gangā on Dashāshvamedh ghat. Each instrument has 108 little flames

105. a) & b) A pūjārī is doing the night pūja on Dashāshvamedh ghat. It is a gift for the gods. Fire of the Kapūrdānī (this instrument) is used to heat the sleep of the Gods c) A pūjārī blows into the conch (shankha) and rings the bell to call the gods, to make music for them and to pacify their sleep

106. Women praying at night at the Śūlatankeshvara temple on Dashāshvamedh ghat

107. Women are praying for the festival of Dālā Chath (Kārttik). They make offerings and install 6 sugar cane sticks (called īkh), connected to the top like a tepee. On the ground it forms a circle around which one installs small lights (diyā), flowers etc...The women sit around this construction to pray and sing "bhajans" (religious songs). Many of these women are coming from Bihar, for the festival

108. Gangā at night. Houses and palaces reflect themselves on the river. Some lights of the Dīvālī festival are still lit

PILGRIMAGE

"By walking one can experience the idea of humanity (pilgrims) and divinity (spirit of the Earth), and by this "unification", one experiences the harmony and transcendence of the pilgrimage—which is ultimately a transcendence of the cosmos in which human beings are at the centre" ("Banāras region" of Rana P.B Singh and Pravin S. Rana). The pilgrims coming from everywhere to Kāshī have the choice between five different pilgrimages (Yātrā). One of the most popular is the Panchakroshi. It delimits the sacred territory of Kāshī and covers a distance of (55.2 miles), 88.5 km. It can be walked on foot, which would take five days. Another choice is to travel by bus or by rickshaw. The pilgrims stop to sleep overnight in rest houses called dharmashālas—some 44 of them. There are 108 altars and temples along the way. 108 is a lucky number in Hindu mythology, being the product of the twelve signs of the Zodiac and the nine planets. The devotees offer five different kind of grains (barley, rice, corn, lentils and black beans), white sesame, bael patra or are bilva leaves (orange tree of the Mālābār) and sacred basil (Tulsī).

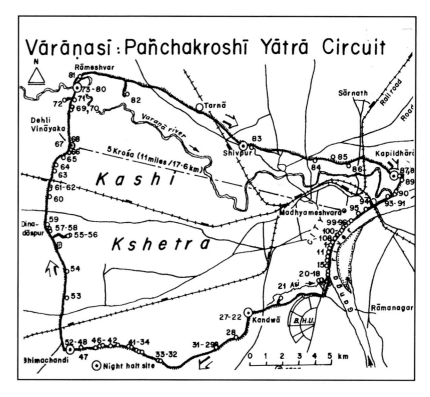

Leaving home, they take only those few things they can carry, and their life is the simple life of the road. Their destinations are spiritual ones, and they are often difficult to reach. Going on foot to a distant place becomes for these pilgrims a kind of asceticism in which the journey itself is as purifying as the sacred destination." (Diana L. Eck in "Banāras city of light").

147

The pilgrimage was, a long time ago, the only reason for the Hindus to travel. Since the arrival of modern means of transport, such as trains and buses, there are yearly a million of pilgrims.

Chardham Yātrā is the pilgrimage to the sources of Ganges and its tributaries. It has to be made in order of the relevance of the places: Gangotrī (the source of Ganges), Yamunotri (the source of Yamunā), Kedārnāth, Badrīnāth.

The cities that welcome the Kumbha melā (gathering which takes place every three years, it is a twelve-years cycle) are, alternatively: Nāsik (Mahārāshtra), Ujjain (Madhya Pradesh), Allāhābād, and Haridvār (Uttar Pradesh).

Holy Cities: Vārānasī, (Uttar Pradesh), Haridvār (Uttar Pradesh), Ayodhyā (Uttar Pradesh), Rāma's birthplace, Mathura (Uttar Pradesh) Krishna's birthplace, Dvārkā (Gujerāt), the place where Krishna becomes is crowned as a king, Kānchipuram (Tāmil Nādu), and Ujjain (Madhya Pradesh).

The pilgrimage to these four cities is the holiest one—it has four divine dwellings, located on the four cardinal points of India's mythological map:

Badrīnāth, in the north, close to the source of the Ganges, associated with Shiva.

Puri (Orissa) in the east, associated with Jagannāth, representations of Krishna.

Rāmeshvaram, (Tāmil Nādu) in the south, associated with Rāma.

Dvārkā, in the west, associated with Krishna.

A city like Banāras is organised upon the pilgrimage and the pilgrim. There are priests who officiate at each stage of the pilgrimage, such as the karmakāndīs, the priests who contribute in particular to the rites, the ghātiās, the priests of a slightly lower range who exert along the ghāts, the pūjārīs, who officiate in the temples, and the mahāpātras, who specialize in the rites of death.

The pilgrims reach Kāshī by foot, by rickshaw or by train; they settle in the resthouses, reserved to the pilgrims, the dharmashālas. They descend the narrow streets, avoid the cows respectfully, bow before the temples, join the ghāts and the river to make their ablutions, they go back up the stairs carrying a small water flask containing sacred water, to be used for the domestic worshiping. Since their childhood, these pilgrims have heard about Kāshī through a sort of traditional literature called the māhātmya. The city is thus not completely unfamiliar for them so they go around there in groups with great ease. Some, barefoot, others carrying a large bag containing their provisions on their head, walking along the river and climbing back the strait paths following a very precise route.

The pilgrim must stop at five holy spots, which are known for being the ones that offer more merits. They are called the Panchatīrthīs: Asi ghāt, Panchagangā ghāt, Dashāshvamedh ghāt, Manikarnikā ghāt, and Ādi Keshava ghāt.

Kāshī is the whole world, they say. Everything on earth that is powerful and auspicious is here, in this microcosm. All of the sacred places of India and all of her sacred waters are here. All of the gods reside here, attracted by the brilliance of the City of Light. All of the eight directions of the compass originated here. To do a pilgrimage to Kāshī is one of the most relevant worships in the life of a Hindu.

RITES AND PŪJĀS

RITES

Life is contemplated as a rite: In the Hindu concept of existence, there is no difference between the sacred actions and the profane activities. The whole life of manhood is a participation in the cosmic symphony. There is no such thing as a meaningless action. All our gestures and all our acts have consequences. They must thus be regulated to match the harmonious drawing of the Universe.

All the day-to-day activities are ritualised: bathing, cooking the meals, the dress code, studying, breathing, love and procreation. These rituals mark the course of the day, the course of the seasons, the course of life. There are rites for every stage of existence: "for his acts, having worshiped the Gods, the man has reached the Liberation" (Bhagavad-Gītā). These rites relate to fire and water. All our acts are apprehended in the form of worships. They must be carried out with serenity and meticulousness, in a well-defined way. In Sanskrit, there is no difference between the physical and the ritual action.

During the pūjā, the devotees perform a well-defined set of gestures: they decorate pictures (Mūrti), place incense, arrange flowers, draw diagrams (Yāntrās), light lamps to whirl them around in the air following a mystic choreography. The worship of the gods goes through the invocation of sacred formulas called "mantras". The ritual must imitate beauty. Then the ritual becomes an art. The daily action merges with the symbolic action.

After having addressed the god, the devotee venerates his image by using fire, flowers, incense, offerings and water, they represent the five elements:

flowers = Ether
lights = Fire
incense = Air
water = Water
food = Earth.

PRIVATE RITES

Each Hindu must perpetuate his family lineage by giving the family at least a son in order to perpetuate the tradition. The first ritual relates to birth with the insertion of a pellet of clarified butter (ghī) and honey into the child's

150

mouth. On their tenth day, the choice of the first name is also an important event and nothing is left to chance. He will even receive a secret name. At the age of four months, they will be considered ready to go out for the first time and they shall be presented to Sūrya (Sun God) in an unchanged ceremonial. With six months it is time for their first solid food, they will eat rice. This meal itself will be also ritualised. Then will come the day, around the age of three, when their hair is cut for the first time.

They are left with only a little tuft of hair on top of the scalp. Then, their ears will be pierced. For the eight to twelve years-old Brahmins, the "initiation" ceremony (Upanayana) will mark their entry in the community as if it was a second birth. The child is granted the "dvija" title, meaning born twice, and they will placed in a three-wire holy cotton rope (Janeū) so that it rests on the left shoulder. The child then begins the true life of a Brah-

man. A private tutor (or guru) is allocated to him, and the child subsequently begins the time taking learning of the holy texts. All these rites, marking the relevant stages of life, are called samskāra. This ceremony is also given importance by the other higher castes who too have the right to learning the scriptures.

WORSHIP RITES

The rite is used to create bonds between this and other worlds. Thus, humans can obtain help from the divinities, who will guide them in their material or spiritual endeavours.

The rites put our world and the gods' world on the same wavelength. They are used to create harmony between gods and humans. They connect the macro-cosmos to the micro-cosmos. A divine dialogue is established and the dimensions of the Universe get closer to those of the humans' world. Using gestures, sounds, songs, rhythms, incense offerings, lights or food, the devotees join the realm of the gods. They reach a spiritual dimension that would be inaccessible for them to reach without these rituals. In a movement of beauty, the man and the gods draw close together and resound in harmony. The symbolism involved in these rituals seems always somewhat obscure for a Westerner, but even if the Hindu devotee does not always know all the meanings, he does know all the forms perfectly. There are two types of rituals: individual worships (pūjā), and ritual sacrifices (Yajnā).

THE LINGAM

The lingam or linga is an upright stone, often of a phallic shape, the traditional representation of Shiva. There are more than 3,000 of them in Vārānasī alone.

There are in fact two types of linga: the "linga made by human hands" and the one "born from itself", i.e., a

natural element venerated as a linga, such as certain pebbles.

The lingam, always standing upright and thus potentially creative, is often associated with the yoni, a symbol of the vulva. In this case, their union represents, together with the image of Shiva, the totality of the world. The phallus, the emblem of Shiva, is divided into three parts. The lowest part, called the Immense one (Brahmā) is square. The second part, which is octagonal, is clasped

152

by Yoni. It is called Immanen (Vishnu). The third part—a cylindrical one—rises above Yoni and is called the Lord of the Tears (Rudra). Undertaking the creative duties of the lingam and the destroying ones in Trimūrti, Shiva represents the god par excellence for the Shiva worshipers, the shivaltes.

There is a great variety of lingams, in sizes and shapes, in all the temples or places devoted to Shiva, from the simple pebble in balance and bearing the painted sign of Shiva to the clearly represented phallus, bearing the carved head of the god.

During the pūjā—the prayer—the lingam is sprinkled with milk, honey or clarified butter (ghī), which is also used for cooking. He is also offered flowers, fruit and sweets. The lingams that are being used must be kept wet.

Like Shiva, the lingam is not mentioned in Vedas though there is mention of Rudra who is later associated with Shiva. Most probably it is a pre-vedic symbol used by the Dravidian and aboriginal tribes that originaly inhabited the sub-continent. It was adopted by the Aryans later as they slowly integrated and absorbed thelocal customs and practices into the larger aspect of their religious practices.

LINGAMS OF LIGHT

Among all the lingams of India, twelve of them are regarded as lingams of light or jyotirlingam and are particularly sacred. One of them is located at the Temple of Vishvanāth, in Kāshī. They are also found in: Somnāth, in Gujarat—the original temple was destroyed during the Muslim invasions; Mallikārjuna in Srisailam—232 km away in the south of Hyderābād; Omkareshvar, in Madhya Pradesh on the banks of the Narmadā; Amareshvara in Ujjain, in Madhya Pradesh; Vaidyanāth in Deogarh in Bihār; Bhīma shankar close to Pune in Mahārāshtra; Rāmeshvaram in Tāmil Nādu; Nāgeshvara in Mahārāshtra; Triambaka close to Nasik and the sources of the Gomatī in Mahārāshtra; Kedārnāth in Uttar Pradesh at an altitude of 3,600 m in the Himalayas; and Grishneshvara in Mahārāshtra close to the caves of Ellorā.

THE MĀLĀ

The mālā (word meaning garland) is a rosary used by the Hindus and the Buddhists for the recitation of the mantras. It is traditionally made with 108 grains, seeds or wood pearls of various essences, sandalwood tulasi and rudraksha for example. 108 is a sacred number because it is the product of the twelve zodiac signs and the nine planets. However, certain sects use some mālās with a lower number of beads. The manufacturing of these mālās is the work of specialized craftsmen called the mālākāras. They are themselves a caste and master of what is regarded as one of the sixty-four

Indian traditional arts. The word mālākāra is for that matter a common surname in Bengal for the craftsmen of this caste.

The mālā is also a garland of flowers (marigold, jasmine etc.) used for offering and for decoration. When placed on a divine icon, it has a devotional meaning.

In the temples, on the ghāts, in the public places, it is not rare to come across men reciting their mantras, their right hand hidden in a fabric glove so that they can use the rosary (mālā) without being seen. Indeed, the prayer is an intimate act and must not be performed at the sight of others. Only one finger, the index one representing the ego sticks out of the glove, symbolizing the fact that in the prayer there is no place for the ego.

THE MANTRAS

In Hinduism and Buddhism, the mantra (Sanskrit "sacred formula") is an intellectual formula or a whole set of syllables put in a certain order, which is repeated many times following a rhythmical pattern. "Man" means "to think". Manu, the "Legislator", the author of the laws of Manu (Mānava-dharmashāstra) was the first one to teach them to humans.

A mantra aims at taking away the distraction and confusion of the mind. It often goes together with the use of a mālā, a kind of rosary with 108 beads.

The most sacred and powerful mantra is the syllable AUM ("I bow over", "I agree", "I accept"). It is regarded as the source of all mantras. "A" represents Brahmā or the terrestrial world, "U" represents Vishnu or the intermediate world, the "M" represents Shiva or the celestial world. AUM is the syllable that precedes the recitation of all mantras. The syllable AUM "contains the whole world. It is the past, the present, the future". (Māndukya Upanishad 1,1.). AUM backs away fear. It must be repeated 108 times or five repetitions, three times each day.

The number of mantras is almost unlimited. There are at least seventy million of them regarded as the main ones. The number of syllables contained in the mantra follows the symbolism of the number: five syllables for the mantras are dedicated to Shiva, eight to Vishnu, twelve are dedicated to the Sūrya Sun-god.

One of the most well known mantras is the Pancakshara: AUM! Namah Shivāya (Aum! I greet Shiva).

Gayatri Mantra (the guardian of the vital energies), which can be heard at all the ghāts as a sign of homage to the god Sun: AUM! Bhūr Bhuvah Svah! Tat Savitur Varenyam Bhargo Devasya Dhīmahi, Dhiyo Yo Nah Pracodayat. AUM!

Lord, we behold your light that fills the three worlds, and pray for your radiance to illuminate our minds.

This mantra must not be pronounced by women or by the low caste men. It must be repeated twelve times.

THE YANTRAS

The Yantras are geometrical figures representing the gods. These diagrams have the same value as their associated mantras. They can be used in all types of worships. One calls upon the divinity and pronounces the mantra while drawing the diagram. These figures express the inner as-

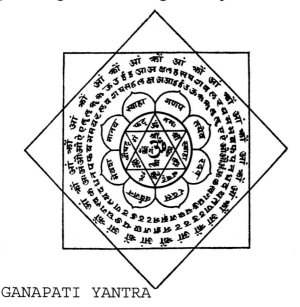

GANAPATI YANTRA

pect of all creation: nature, men, animals, and Gods. They are considered very powerful and are one of the most secretly kept forms of Hindu esoteric teaching.

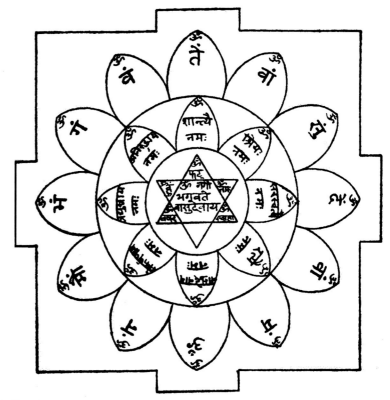

VISHNU YANTRA

The dot (bindu) is a spatial concept, the symbol of the Ether, and represents movement and form. The straight line represents the movement without obstacle, the development. The igneous triangle (which has the shape of a flame), the flame, the arrow tip represents the male aspect. The aqueous triangle (in opposite direction of the igneous triangle), the wave, the circle arc or crescent symbolize the passive aspect of creation, the inertia, the yoni, the female principle, it is a symbol of energy

155

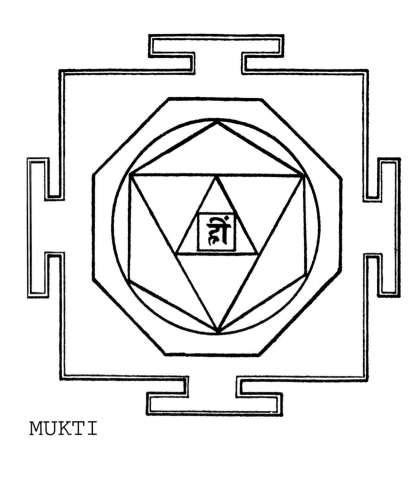

MUKTI

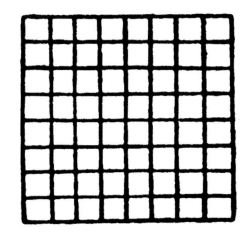

SARVATO-BHADRA

SHRI YANTRA

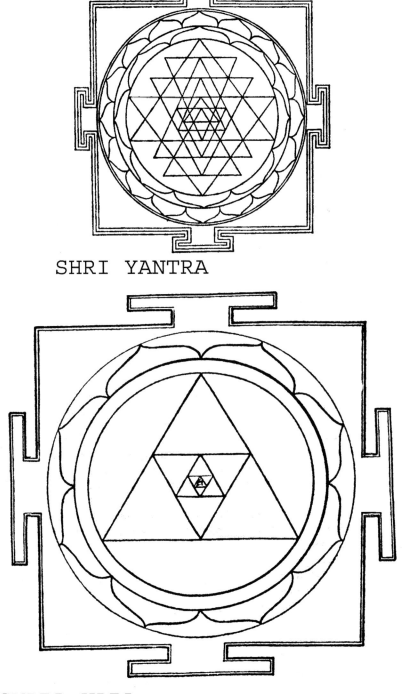

SMARA-HARA

YANTRA RAJA

(shakti). The circle depicts the stars' revolution and symbolizes everything that returns to its starting point all that is cyclic, thus pointing to the cycle of the existence. The hexagon, the pentagon or the square—representing the Earth—are there, too. Also the cross, regarded as a dot that develops in space stretches in the four directions. The swastika is also found, a symbol of happy predictions, also generated from a dot (bindu) and developing into the four directions. The star-studded hexagon, formed by an igneous triangle and an aqueous triangle is a six-pointed star and represents the universe. These same two triangles placed one on top of the other as an hourglass symbolize time. The well-known shape of the lotus is also commonly found.

All these shapes combined with one another form the yantra, whose meaning can be very variable. Their symbolism is particularly interesting albeit somewhat obscure for the secular. Their forms alone are an invitation to an inner journey.

TEMPLES (MANDIRS)

VISHVANĀTH TEMPLE

The temple of Vishvanāth is dedicated to Shiva. It is the holiest and most visited temple of Kāshī. In 1835, Mahārāja Ranjit Singh (of Punjāb) provided the 820 kilos of gold, which nowadays cover its 15.5 meter-high dome, giving it the nickname "Golden Temple". The exact date of its construction is unknown, but it is at least 1300 years old, as it is mentioned by the Chinese monk Hiuen Tsiang in the 7th century C.E. Several invaders throughout history had destroyed this temple but by far the most famous as well as the last amongst them being the Mughal emperor Aurangzeb, who ordered the destruction of the temple in 1669. He converted it into a mosque. The temple was rebuilt in 1776-1777 by Rani Ahilyābāī of Indore. The

Gyanvapi mosque, built by Aurangzeb after destroying the temple, still stands close to the temple of Vishvanāth quite obviously on the original site.

The pilgrims who pass through Kāshī must go to the temple of Vishvanāth. All around the temple and in the numerous and tiny lanes (gali) leading to the temple, there are countless merchants of flowers and other objects of worship. The smell of jasmine and marigold of which the garlands are made of (which shall be used for the worships) impregnates the air in the whole area. The offerings of flowers (pushpa), sweets (naivedya) and water of the Ganges (Gangājala) fill up the stalls of the small merchants. The temple's main door is covered in silver. The pilgrims go into a large rectangular court, in whose centre is the temple itself. On the side, there is a two-metre-high statue representing the bull Nandī, the vehicle of Shiva and adored as such. It symbolizes justice and uprightness. But the most attractive place for the pilgrims is the famous and much venerated lingam of light, jyotirlingam. (There are only twelve light lingams—jyotirlingam—all over India, and they are particularly adored). It is sprinkled with water from the Ganges, anointed with sandalwood paste, mixed with bhāng (cannabis), honey, ghī (clarified butter) and milk. It is completely covered with jasmine flowers, roses and marigold, bilva leaf (bael, orange tree of Mālābār) called bael patra. During the ceremonies (āratī), the sound of the bells, the conches, the songs, the recitations of the mantras, as well as the incense fragrance (dhoop) and the fervour of the pilgrims give these places an atmosphere of intense devotion.

Jnanavapi Kupa is not far from the temple; it is a well whose water is supposed to lead to a higher level of consciousness and to wisdom. Entry to the temple is prohibited to non-Hindus.

ANNAPŪRNĀ BHAVĀNĪ TEMPLE

After praying in the temple of Vishvanāth, the pilgrims go towards the Annapūrnā Bhavānī temple located nearby. Annapūrnā is the goddess of abundance (goddess of plenitude of food). Bhavā meaning "being" is one of the names of Shiva, its female force, called "the mother of the three worlds". This temple was built by Balaji Bajirao Peshva in 1725. It has a tower and a dome decorated in the purest Hindu style. Just after the festival of Divālī, the Annakūta festival takes place, during which the devout people make offerings to the goddess of abundance. Enormous quantities of fruit, sweets and cereals are then placed on the temple before being distributed to the poor.

DURGĀ TEMPLE (MONKEY TEMPLE)

The temple of Durgā, with its the immense pond (Kund), is one of the most important places of Kāshī. It was built in the 18th century in nagara style by the queen Rani

Bhavānī of Natore (Bengal). But it was already a holy place well before that date, since one finds traces of this location in the 12th century Kāshī khanda writings. At

the beginning of the 20th century, it was still surrounded by jungle. It can be accessed through two different en-

tries. The temple itself is located in the centre of a rectangular courtyard and is supported up by twelve splendid carved pillars. The Hindus ring the bells there. One such bell was offered to the temple by William James Grant after being saved from drowning by a boatman who had just implored the Goddess Durgā to help him. Every Tuesday and Saturday, many Hindus go there to pray and sing bhajans (hymns), creating a spellbinding atmosphere. Durgā is one of the most worshiped goddesses in the north of India. People go there to worship and see (darshana) Durgā's silver mask, which is covered with a red fabric cloth. Sacrifices of goats take place there during the month of Chaitra (March-April). Flowers, sweets and other items for offering are sold by vendors sitting at the entrances of the temple.

TULSĪ MĀNAS TEMPLE

The modern-styled temple of Tulsī Mānas located not far from the Temple of Durgā is dedicated to Rāma. It

was built in 1963 entirely out of marble. All the verses of the famous Rāmacharitramānas epic written by the poet Tulsī Dās who lived in Kāshī (1532-1623), are engraved on the walls. The Rāmacharitramānas is the Hindi version of Rāmāyana, relating the adventures of Rāma. A collection of issues of the famous work is found on the second floor. Then there are several scenes of the epic Rāmāyana put on stage with puppets and robots, mostly enjoyed by children but also by all Indians who know each scene by heart and remain fascinated with these animations. The temple is surrounded by a large garden featuring statues representing scenes from Indian mythology.

SANKAT MOCHAN TEMPLE

At the end of the 16th century, the poet Tulsī Dās (1532-1623) installed under a tree, an immense pīpal (ficus religiosa—holy fig tree), an image of Lord Hanumāna (the monkey god) to whom the temple is now dedicated. Hundreds of monkeys have made their homes in the vicinity. Hanumāna is the god who eases troubles (liberator from troubles). It is one of the three places most visited by Banārsīs, along with the Vishvanāth and Annapūrnā temples. The inhabitants of Kāshī are very attached to this temple where they come in multitudes for their worshipping and their darshana (vision), mainly on Tuesdays and Saturdays. They go there to make their offerings, pray and sing. A peaceful atmosphere reigns in the large courtyard. Married couples go there to receive blessings and a concert to celebrate the birth of Hanumāna in the month of Chaitra (March-April) take place at the site.

BHĀRAT MĀTĀ TEMPLE

This temple is devoted to Mother India (Bhārat Mātā Mandir). It is located 1.5 kilometres away from the Vārānasī station. It was inaugurated by Mahātma Gāndhi in 1936. 20 craftsmen carved the huge marble map of India reproducing the country in three dimensions featuring its mountains, its valleys, its oceans and its pilgrimage routes over a period of six years.

NEPĀLĪ TEMPLE

This temple was built under the patronage of a Nepalese king in the surroundings of the Lalitā ghāt. It is built in the purest Nepalese style. Made out of bricks and wood, it is also known as "Kathwala". With its pagoda roof, it represents Nepalese architecture and was built by Nepalese craftsmen who brought the wood from Nepal that cannot be eaten by the termites. It is possible to enjoy a splendid view of the Ganges under the shade

of a huge tree, where agitated naughty monkeys fidget and, sometimes, lost kites cling to it. Much frequented by Nepalese, Bhutanese or the inhabitants of Sikkim, it is a calm place where young Sanskrit students and old women come to chat or make their pūjā around a lingam, simmilar to the one in Kathmandu. Its guardian kindly welcomes the visitors. The woodwork of the temple is finely carved in the newari style, sometimes with erotic motifs. It is a serene place.

KEDĀRANATH TEMPLE

The legend goes that this temple had survived the massive destruction carried out by the Mughal Emperor Aurangzeb. It can therefore be considered more ancient than the celebrated and venerated temple of Vishvanāth. One enters it through a small door leading from the street

or from the ghāt bearing the same name. From the riverbank, it is easy to spot it thanks to its saffron and white vertical stripes and its steep stairs. The visitors are mainly inhabitants of southern India or Bengalis. Some

of them are pilgrims, others live in the neighbourhood. There are references to this temple in the very ancient Purāna manuscripts. On Mondays, Shiva is enthusiastically worshipped and yet the atmosphere is calm and full of fervour. The lingam there is particularly adored, for it would not have been made by human hands—it rather would be a spontaneous revelation of Shiva itself.

KĀLA BHAIRAVA TEMPLE

Going back up from the Panchaganga ghāt and following the small lanes (gali) one walks in front of this temple

dedicated to Kāla Bhairava (one of the scarring shapes of Shiva) without even catching a glimpse of it. A few vendors of flowers and of offerings, a statue of a

dog, Kāla Bhairava's vehicle (vāhana) and the fervour of the worshipers lead the way there. This temple, built under the patronage of the Maratha king Bajirao Peshva II in 1817, is one of the most interesting places in the city. Bhairava is worshiped to obtain protection, health and well being, but not to be liberated. Some priests bless the passing pilgrims using peacock feathers and putting black thread necklaces around their necks.

MAHĀ MRITYUNJAYA TEMPLE

A gate with fine silver sculptures adorns the entrance. Against the right-hand side wall, a row of men recite their mantras with a mālā, a rosary in the hand—hidden by a cloth glove—while on the left, people gather around the effigies to make their offerings. Further away, a courtyard is illuminated by a soft light and there is an atmosphere of meditation and out-of-time fervour. Seeing the serenity of this place, it is difficult to imagine that Mrityunjaya is the conqueror of death.

NEW VISHVANĀTHA TEMPLE

Built in 1962 with the financial support of the wealthy Birla family (hence also called "Birla Mandir") this white-marble temple sits imposingly in the centre of the huge Banāras Hindu University campus, (BHU). It was built imitating the style of the Vishvanātha temple, destroyed by Aurangzeb. The verses of old writings (Veda, Purāna and the complete Bhagavad Gītā), decorate its walls. It

is open to everyone. Its dome, the 76.50m high shikhara, can be seen from any point of the whole campus.

MĀ ĀNANDAMAYĪ ĀSHRAM

Located not far from the Asi ghāt, the Āshram of Mā Ānandamayī majestically overlooks the Ganges and the ghāt, which bears its name. Mā Ānandamayī is regarded as a great wise woman and is one of the most respected spiritual Masters known in modern India. This woman, born in 1896 in Bengal and died in 1982, had a really intense lifetime. Her teachings found in her many

Āshrams throughout the country have made her both venerated and popular. The Kāshī Āshram is vast and

includes several buildings, one dharmashāla (resthouse) for the hosts, one large courtyard with trees and flowers, two temples, a sunny terrace, and a stairway that leads down to the river. It is a place for education, for instruction, spiritual training and meditation.

THE SĀDHUS

The Hindus consider that the ultimate goal in life is the moksha, the liberation, the end of the rebirth cycle and the dissolution within the divine, and the fusion with the cosmic consciousness. This objective is rarely attained during the lifetime.

The sādhus (from the Sanskrit "man of good, holy man") choose to lead a life of austerity in order to accelerate this process, to reach this status at the end of this life. The sādhus have been present in India for several thousands of years—maybe since prehistory—where their role was similar to that of a Shaman. In the 5th century BC, Buddha joined them at one point in his search for illumination. They are the gymnosophists, the naked philosophers that the Greeks of Alexander the Great once came across with when he arrived in the Indian

world. It seems that their number largely increased in the 13th century. General estimations count them as a 0.5 % of the Indian population.

The sādhus are abnegators. They cut every bond with their family, do not posses anything or very little, they wear a loin cloth, (symbolizing holiness), saffron-colour in the case of the shivaḷtes, yellow or white for the vaishnavites, and sometimes strings of beads or rosaries around their necks. They do not have a roof and spend their lives moving on the roads of India and Nepal, being fed by the devotees' donations.

In their search for the Absolute, the sādhus practise the tapas (austerities), mantra recitations, magic rituals, breath control, yoga to unify body and soul, celibacy, vow of silence, meditation or mortifications. These very mortifications that the Buddha refused to define his Middle Way. The practice of tapas is supposed to increase spiritual energy allowing them to reach an almost divine status. The sexual energy being a major source of this spiritual energy, abstinence allows to increase it.

A great number of them consume hash ritually, as Shiva is supposed to do, to tear the veil of the māyā (illusion). For them, it is tolerated by the Indian State who, however, prohibits its use by law. Other sādhus refuse its consumption, which they judge to be against their ideals.

The shaivaite sādhus rub their bodies with ashes, symbols of death and rebirth. Imitating Shiva, they have extremely long hair in dreadlocks, which have been adopted by the Rastafarians.

The allegiance of the sādhus to Shiva or Vishnu is recognized by the traditional marks they paint on their foreheads and sometimes by the colour of their clothes. During the Kumbha melā they may confront one another, each one trying to be the first to enter the holy water.

Besides the desire for spiritual research, the original reasons which make a sādhu choose that way of life can be very diverse: to escape their caste—because the holy men do not recognize castes—to flee from a painful family situation, to go away from a calamitous financial situation, but there are also women avoiding the infamy of widowhood. That is why there are sādhu women or sādhvīs (10% of the sādhus population), even if there are only very few young ones, in contrast with the males: there are the chelas, the sādhus' male pupils, who can be very young.

IMPORTANT SĀDHU SECTS:

NĀGAS

The Nāgas ("naked") form a shaivite sect of ascetic warriors exist since about 550C.E., and, as opposed to the other sādhus, they are vindicatory, organized into seven akhārās, i.e., in regiments, and get easily in conflict with the other sects. They even fought militarily against the Muslims and later against the English. They often carry weapons nowadays rather in a symbolic way—such as swords, sticks, spears and, above all, the trident, a sign of Shiva.

As their name indicates, they often wear no clothes. They are specialists in the mortification of their penis, often attaching very heavy weights to it with the purpose of desexualising themselves. This practice was attested by the Abbot Dubois, one of the first experts on India.

KĀNPHATĀS

The Kānphatā or "Nath babas" follow the tantra teachings of the Gorakhnath sect founded around the year 1000. They regard Baba Gorakhnath as an incarnation of Shiva and who is the traditional author of the first treatise of Hatha Yoga Pradipika. Their sect is supposed to be as old as the world. Brahmā, Vishnu and Shiva were the first disciples of Gorakhnath, immediately after the creation. The Kānphatās bear the kundala, an earring, where the ear is pierced during a strongly ritualised ceremony. They pray also to Hanumāna and Dattātreya. Their main centre is Gorakhpur in Uttar Pradesh.

UDASINS

The Udasin ascetics, or Nanak's children, are neither the followers of Shiva, nor of a Hindu origin, as they belong to the Sikh religion. The sect was founded by Shrichandra, the son of Guru Nanak, founder of Sikhism, and its members venerate him as well as the panchāyatana, a group of five divinities: Shiva, Vishnu, Sūrya, Durgā and Ganesh, since they turned to Hinduism when the second guru Sikh excommunicated them. In the event of a possible conflict between sects, they take sides with the Shaivites.

RĀMĀNANDIS

The Rāmānandis are a sect that was established based on the teachings of the philosopher Rāmānanda (15th century). They are also called Vairāgīs—those indifferent to the world—and Avadhūta—those who renounced everything. They practise the bhakti of Rāma and Sītā.

AGHORĪS

The Aghorīs are the most extremist of all the sādhu sects. Kina Ram, an ascetic of the 18th century, was the founder. They seek illumination by following Shivas' behaviours, the ones that challenge the norms to the furthest extreme. There are only a few of them nowadays, some twenty who live in Vārānasī, close to the grave of their guru, but their number must have been much larger in the past, probably 200 to 300 at the end of the 19th century.

As opposed to the other ascetics, as well as to most Hindus, they are not vegetarians and consume alcohol. Imitating Shiva, they live at the cremation areas, naked or draped in a shroud. They are credited with having practices of absolute impurity, like consuming decomposing meat, eating their own excrement and urine, meditating on top of dead corpses, and copulating with prostitutes during menstruation. In this last case, it would be a Tantra rite to get reincarnated-together with their partners—in Shiva and Kālī. In fact, Aghorīs think that the extremes are identical and that the traditional Hindu distinction between pure and impure is just an illusion they want to be released from. They enjoy being surrounded by symbols of death, especially by human craniums, which they use as drinking vessels and as ritual instruments.

THE UNIVERSITIES

BANĀRAS HINDU UNIVERSITY: BHU

It is the largest and oldest University of North India. The campus of the BHU, as it is usually known, is located five km from the railway station to the south of the city. It is the largest university campus of India. It originates from the Central Hindu College founded by Annie Besant. But it was on February 14th 1916, when Madan Mohan Mālavīya gave it the scope known today and created the Banāras Hindu University. Stretching out in a 1370 acre (554.5 ha) half-circle, symbolizing Shiva's half-moon-shaped forehead, one enters it through a large gate, as in a temple. That is the way Pandit Madan Mohan Mālavīya conceived it, hence it is known as the Temple of Knowledge. There are not less than 124 diploma courses, 14 faculties featuring 3 Institutes

of agronomy, medicine and technology with 1,800 professors, 15,000 students and 7,000 non-academic employees. This University attracts students not only from all over India but also from other Asian countries as well as countries all over the world.

It intends to be the reflection of the image always mirrored by Kāshī, i.e. a land of knowledge, the centre of learning that the city, throughout its history, has always been, attracting, since the dawn of time, the greatest poets, thinkers, the finest musicians…Buddha (6th century BC), Mahavira (599-527 BC), the last of the Tirthankaras of the Jaïn religion, the poet Tulsī Dās (1532-1623), Rāmānanda, Kabir (1440-1518), Ravi Shankar, the sitar player (born in 1920 near Kāshī) to mention but a few of them. The University shelters the Bhārat Kalā Bhavan Museum, which contains very beautiful collections of sculptures, paintings, manuscripts, etc…It also shelters the new temple of Vishvanātha, financed by the Birla family. It is open to everyone, regardless of caste or religion.

THE SANSKRIT UNIVERSITY

Kāshī has always been a land of knowledge. Since the most ancient times the pandits (erudite Brahmans) had been teaching the holy texts. The knowledge was transmitted orally from teacher to disciple. At the time, the Language of Knowledge was Sanskrit. In 1791 Jonathan Duncan thus created the Sanskrit College. The Gothic building, which was erected in 1853 may still be found there. All subjects are

taught in Sanskrit, including non-literary subjects. Astrology, astronomy, religion, philosophy, languages, and ayurvedic medicine...are also taught there. Its Sanskrit name is: Vārānaseya Sanskrit Vishvavidyālaya, which means "Sankrit of Vārānasī, Ocean of All The Learnings". The College became a University in 1958. Its library, "Sarasvatī Bhavana" is famous worldwide because

it holds the world's largest collection of manuscripts in Sanskrit language. These manuscripts are priceless and the knowledge contained within represents the heart of the cultural, religious, philosophical and artistic heritage of the Indian civilisation. The entrance to the premises is authorized only under very strict conditions.

SANSKRIT

The Sanskrit is read from left to right. Its alphabet is a literal alphabet. It originates from the Veda languages whose existence is attested approximately in the middle of the second millennium BC. The San-

skrit language, during centuries, was simply known as sabda, "the word, the language", Sanskrit being perceived as the only possible language. From its birthplace in the North-West of India, over a period of possibly four millennia, Sanskrit spread throughout Asia to the East of Iran. In India, Sanskrit is used all over the Indo-Gangetic plain. Its expansion to the remaining areas of India occurred after the Christian era.

The origin of the group of Indo-European languages is believed to be India and has thus been dubbed Indo-Aryan.

There are three different periods namely: —

The "old Indo-Aryan", which is the language of the Vedas, which has survived until today thanks to classic Sanskrit.

The "middle Indo-Aryan" is a group of languages derived from the ancient form (example: Pali from Buddhist writings, Ardhamāgadhī from the Jaina writings, literary pākrits, from the inscriptions…)

The "modern Indo-Aryan", consisting of several languages which, generating from these multiple roots, diversified over the Indian territory and are the great living languages in most of the northern Indian States.

Note: "Indo-Aryan" is slightly different to the "Dravidian", another great family of the Indian languages (Tamil, Kannada, Telugu, and Malayalam etc…) in the southern states of the peninsula which were supposedly the languages of the original inhabitants of the sub-continent..

SPOKEN SANSKRIT

We only know the literary works by poets and experts of the religious practice. It is probable that the Veda language found in the writings is dissociated from the popular speech. However there is no document on this particular.

In the absence of written documents, the very first transmission of the Vedas was oral, from Teacher to disciple, by word of mouth, the quality of transmission depending on the human memory. Veda, literally "to know", is also called, Śruti "hearing".

Recitation is the determining factor to safeguard the language. The only text of the Rig Veda contains 10,462 verses and 153,826 words. The oral training for the continuous recitation (samkitā) alone lasts two years. To learn the eleven recitations takes a dozen years, starting at the age of 6-8. Then, recitation becomes a profession. The first duty of the person who recites is to teach it since the aim of recitation is to ensure the ongoing transmission of the teachings. On the other hand, a religious value is attached to it. It is a rite carried out at home, on certain occasions. It is still an actual living rite in our times and the profession is still practiced. It is impossible not to notice the success the oral transmission of the Vedas has had for more than four millennia, even before the appearance of the writing, not too old in India.

The Sanskrit pandit (the Sanskrit erudite) has a liking for oral communication. He disregards the writing. The word, the quality of the speaker is what makes the pandit more popular than the book itself. The great author is the Master who speaks. The ideal model of the creative genius is the mythic figure of the wise man Vyāsa, regarded as the author of Mahābhārata—an epical text of 400,000 octosyllabic verses—and many other works. He delivered the stories from his own mouth. The legend tells us that the task to put this mass of words into writing was entrusted to Ganesha, a god with the body of a child and the head of an elephant, the son of Shiva and Pārvatī.

Another mythical poetical figure is Vālmīki, author of Rāmāyana, which initiates the style of the great classic Sanskrit poetry and it is the foundation of one of the largest trends of the Hindu religion.

WRITTEN SANSKRIT

Sanskrit existed for many centuries before being given a written form. The writing is attested in India by pictograms carved on seals in the valley of the Indus in the 3rd millennium BC. Later on, by two Kharosthi manuscripts in the North West of the country and by the Brahmi in the rest of the country in the 3rd century BC.

The first documents in written Sanskrit date from the first centuries of the Christian era. The massive and regular production of manuscripts is typical of the Middle Age. The writings are made on stone, monument walls, copperplates, palm leaves, and birch bark etc…Finally in the 11th century on paper, whose use becomes common in India at that time. The scribe engraved the letters on a palm tree leave, drew them with the calamus (reed which was used by the ancient people to write) and ink.

The grammar and structure of Sanskrit are particularly complex. The three main grammar experts are: Pānini (500 BC), Kātyāna (mid 3rd century BC), and Pantanjali (2nd century BC). They created works for the study of Sanskrit. The word "Sanskrit" (samskrta)—according to the tradition of the pandits—means the form of speech "built" based in a grammar such as Panini's. The first meaning of samskrta in its common use means "trimmed". Samskrta is what has been prepared for a coming action. It also means "refined, purified, perfect", being thus opposed to the word prākrita meaning "natural, vulgar" and refers to the various popular languages.

The Sanskrit is well known as a religious language, but there's a strong tendency to regard it as nothing else. Moreover, it is not the only religious language in India. It is the language of the old Vedic religion. Sanskrit is also the lingua franca between regions with different languages, within the scientific and the technical languages, as well as the literary language. Bāna Bhatta is one of the greatest geniuses of Sanskrit literature. In a totally independent way, he sang the exploits of the king Harsha (605-647) of Kanyākubja, in the poetical novel "The Epic of Harsha".

The founders of the three main trends of the Sanskrit philosophy are: Samkara (8th century), Rāmānuja (1017-1137?) and Madhva (1238-1317)—the three of them are from the furthest southern regions of the peninsula.

A large number of Indian manuscripts—the majority of them in Sanskrit—are currently kept in India in State libraries and private collections.

LIVING SANSKRIT

Sanskrit is still alive today, but it suffered very serious attacks in modern history. From the 16th century, the great neo-Indian languages have taken over. Then, as from the 17th century, the Muslim domination takes away two of the monopolies held by the Sanskrit: the one as the communicative language and use in diplomacy, and the one as the vehicle of scientific and technical knowledge. Indeed, Persian replaces Sanskrit as the language for internal and foreign relations.

The European colonization had also a severe effect on the Sanskrit. In the beginning of the 19th century, English substitutes Persian. But the tradition of studying Sanskrit was never stopped by colonization. The Sanskrit's main traditional uses do not decline, nor its tuition, its literary production or its religious use.

Independent India will work towards revitalize its traditional culture. Sanskrit is the best representation of the traditional Indian civilisation's unity. There is thus a very strong call to revive this language. Its teaching, study and literary production never stopped. Efforts are currently being made to increase and to maintain this trend. Sanskrit is taught in secondary schools, and in higher study levels it is taught in to more advanced degree. There are several Sanskrit universities (Banāras, Puri, Tirupati etc...) where the teaching of all the main subjects—including scientific studies—is carried out in Sanskrit. There are great study centres of Sanskrit such as the Bhandarka Oriental Research Institute of Poona and many others, without mentioning the private enterprises that aim at re-creating a living and popular use of Sanskrit (Viśva samskrta Pratisthana in Banāras, etc...).

Sanskrit was the language of the educated people, but not the mother tongue of any class. The study of Sanskrit is still alive today. There is the will to preserve this cultural heritage. Sanskrit is not excluded from the main media. There are television broadcasts, made entirely in Sanskrit, such as theatre plays or childrens programmes. On the radio, daily news bulletins are broadcast in Sanskrit all over Indian. There are more than one hundred newspapers in Sanskrit. The literary Sanskrit production increases year after year. Sanskrit is definitely very much alive.

POST-VEDIC HINDU WRITINGS

Mahābhārata: (literally "Greater India") is a Sanskrit Epic from the Hindu mythology, composed of more than one hundred twenty thousand verses. This work can be compared to the Bible for the Christians. It is often regarded as the greatest poem ever made.

It tells the history of a war between the Pāndavas—king Pāndu's children—and the Kauravās—the children of the king Dhritarāshtra's (Pāndu's blind eldest brother)—all members of the warrior caste (kshatriya) in the region of Delhi. Originally, the text was probably a compilation of stories of gods and heroes orally transmitted, performed by theatre companies, told by the priests and the sannyāsis—to the pilgrims—before being compiled and written in a slightly archaic Sanskrit, known as "epic Sanskrit". It was later adapted in the Indian languages and was propagated in South-East Asia at the time of the Indian expansion in the first millennium. The main event of the text is the appearance of Krishna.

The Bhagavad Gītā is an episode included in the sixth book of Mahābhārata. A Masterpiece of the Hindu thinking, it relates the moral advice that Krishna gave to Arjuna, who is in despair having to take part in a battle where many of his friends and relatives are likely to lose their lives and that also by his hand. It is a fundamental text to know about the life of traditional India and it is also a statement of Hindu ideals. Traditionally, the Mahābhārata is supposed to have been written by Ganesha under the dictation of the wise man Vyāsa.

The Mahābhārata is an endless source of inspiration for the Indian performing arts- in particular theatre and cinema.

Rāmāyana: in Sanskrit, "the epic of Rāma", this is the shortest epic in Sanskrit, written between the 3rd century BC and the 3rd century of our era. Consisting of seven books and 48,000 verses, the Rāmāyana is, together with the Mahābhārata, one of the fundamental writings of Hinduism and the Indian civilisation.

The Rāmāyana recounts the birth and the education of prince Rāma. The text also tells of his exile, the abduction of Sītā, her release, and the return of Rāma to the throne.

When he is taken away from his father's throne (although he is the legitimate heir), Rāma exiles himself from Ayodhyā, accompanied by Sītā and his brother Lakshmana. Then Sītā is abducted by the Rāvana demon. After a long and painful search, Rāma freed her with the assistance of Hanumān, the Monkeys' Army general. Rāvana is killed by Rāma, who subsequently recovers his throne and reigns with great wisdom.

The Rāmāyana contains many Vedic stories, but it is not exclusively of a religious nature, for it also contains legends, mythical or cosmological tales (formation of the Earth as seen by the Brahmans). Its recitation bears a worshiping value in Brahmanism and certain scenes are still performed (as in a dancing theatre play of South India named kathakālī). It still remains very popular in today's India.

THE BHAKTI SCHOOLS
(or Devotional philosophy)

Between 1400 and 1650, a great bhakti movement develops in the north of India. The teachings of this movement allow people to get rid of the rituals' heavy burdens, of the caste, and of subtle philosophical complexities, so that they can express their immense love for God in a simple manner.

During this period there was a profusion of worship literature in the vernacular languages (spoken languages) of the various Indian states or provinces. The head of the bhakti movement is Rāmānanda, from Kāshī. He became the guru of Kabīr.

Very little is known about him, but he is supposed to have thrived during the first half of the 15th century. He teaches that Rāma is the supreme lord, and that redemption can only be achieved through love and devotion towards him, and through the repetition of his holy name.

The āshram of Rāmānanda in Vārānasī becomes then an influential religious centre, from which its ideas are absorbed within all the classes of the Indian society. One of the reasons for its great popularity is the abandonment of the Sanskrit in favour of the vernacular languages for the composition of its hymns. This paved the way for Northern India to use local languages to write literary texts.

The development of the bhakti left an indelible trace on the faith. In India as elsewhere, philosophical thinking was always the concern of a minority. The practice of bhakti, however, is immediately accessible to everybody. Even if it does not eliminate the worst characteristics of the castes' system, at least it offers a provisional respite to the people.

KABĪR

Kabīr was a poet, philosopher and the major religious vaishnavite reformer in Northern India. Born in Vārānasī around 1398 and died in Gorakhpur in the year 1440 (the dates concerning his life are arguable, certain sources state dates such as 1440 for his birth and 1518 for his death, in the same way a great number of events are only known via the legends transmitted by his disciples).

This legend affirms that Kabīr was the abandoned son of a Brahman widow, found floating on a lotus flower in Lahar Tara, a pond close to Vārānasī, by a couple of Muslim weavers—Nīru and his wife Nīmā. They brought him up by teaching him their craft and the Muslim faith. He is supposed to have lived the major part of his life in Banāras, before settling down in Maghar, in the district of Gorakhpur, where he finished his life.

Kabīr is supposed to have studied under the direction of Rāmānanda, a famous Vaishnavite Master at that time, an enthusiastic bhakti follower, but who however refuses to educate Muslims and Hindus from lower castes. The legend tells us that, wishing to be admitted as a disciple, Kabīr went to the ghāts where Rāmānanda made his ablutions. Using one of his subterfuges, he manages—by surprise—to make the master pronounce the sacred mantra "Rām" which initiates his future disciple. Following this event, and overjoyed by Kabīr's intelligence, Rāmānanda's mind changes and he starts accepting all sorts of disciples.

At the time, this tendency to syncretise seems common in Northern India. The teachings of the first Sikh gurus were mainly based on his transmitted knowledge. Moreover, he asserts that any religion that is not about love is only heresy, that yoga and penitence, fasting and alms, without meditation, are meaningless. He refutes any distinctions of race, caste or religion and teaches the absolute equality of all human beings. He mixes in his practice Hindu and Muslim elements, declaring the unity of god, using the name of Rāma, who means for him the one who gives us the joy. He also condemned the few sacrifices of animals still practised by the Brahmans as a means of worship, thus following the Buddhist teachings, which had almost made such practices disappear from India. He also advocated vegetarianism.

The rāja of Vārānasī was among his pupils. This allowed him to teach without any fear of persecution. Towards the end of his life, contrary to the Hindu aspirations, he leaves Vārānasī—the city where one must die—to settle in the allegedly cursed area of Gorakhpur (those who die there are supposed to be reincarnated in an ass) to prove that his love for Rāma are more than sufficient to bring him salvation. After his death, Hindus and Muslims claimed his body to practise the funerary rites according to their religion. The legend tells us that, under the shroud, there was only a heap of flowers, which was divided, one part was buried, and the other one was burned.

THE ETERNAL YOGI

Oh Saints, I am a deathless, eternal yogi
I come from nowhere, I go to no place
I am never extinguished.
Always abiding in the heart,
I enjoy the cosmic, unstruck music.

Every place is my home
And wherever I am, a festival, a carnival.
I am in everything, And everything rests within me,
Yet I am absolutely alone.

I am perfection, and I am equilibrium
I am the process, I am the goal
I am silence, and I am sound

By manifesting form and formlessness,
beauty and ugliness
I play within myself

Says Kabīr, listen oh Saints,
I have no desires
I live alone, in my own hut
Created from myself.
My existence is a self-willed
Spontaneous play.

BIRD FROM FOREIGN LAND

Oh Baba, I am a lost bird from a foreign land
I do not belong to this land
In this land, people are asleep and unconscious
Unware that time slips away never to return.
Each moment, a cosmic dissolution.
Oh Saints, I do not belong to this land

In my country, I could sing without a mouth,
Fly without wings, walk without feet
My form had no shape
And I was forever merged with the unstruck
Melody in the heart
Oh Saints, I do not belong to this land

In my true home, my meditation was
Continuous, unbroken, spontaneous and effortless
Where the mind and prana cannot reach,
That is my true home, oh brothers.
My lord and Master has no form, no attributes.
Yet he takes on all forms and all qualities
Says Kabīr, listen Oh Saints
Within me, the whole universe!

(Poems translated from the Hindi by Krishna Kant Shukla)

176

LAL DED OR LALLA

She was born in the 16th century (between 1317 and 1320) in a village from Kashmir in the North of India, from a Brahmin family where she received a good level of education and lived in a very religious atmosphere. She was known as Lal Ded or Lalla.. She was a laywoman and married villager. But when she moved to her husband's village, her mother-in-law cruelly treated her. Caught in the routine of the everyday family life, with no children, and guided by an irresistible call, she committed herself to a spiritual adventure in the tradition of the Trika Shivaism or Kashmiri Shivaism, after having lived a dozen years within her in-law family. She became a "tapasvin" (ascetic) and, intoxicated with God, she renounced everything to live as a hermit. She never left her region, did not preach, did not write and did not transmit any sort of teaching, strictly speaking. Those who listened to her kept her message and transmitted it orally. She challenged conventions, not observing the religious ceremonials, the traditional formulas of piety, openly criticizing the orthodoxy, the dogmas, the rituals, the hypocrisy and the narrow-mindedness, the Sanskrit chroniclers did not think it was good to give her a place in their writings. She always stood apart from the worship forms of popular Hinduism. The recognition of her thinking, similar to the Bhaktis' thinking, was only discovered long after her death in the mid 18th century when interest about her arose. Her reputation was surrounded with legends and miracles. It is said that crowds went to receive her blessings, that she walked naked while dancing and singing in a frantic

ecstasy. She was not concerned with her appearance. Only her innermost soul concerned her. She hated daily sacrifices (yajna), did not practise pūjā and thought that God is in oneself and not one supposedly in the statues or in the symbolic figures.

"The statue is nothing but a stone,
The temple is nothing but a stone,
Everything, from top to bottom, is nothing but a stone".

Lal Ded did not accept any discrimination, lived as a wandering ascetic, engrossed in God, both seeking and seeing God everywhere. It is told that when she died (about 1372) "a sparkling flame left her body and vanished". There is no temple, nor any sign indicating the place where her body could have been burned or buried.

CASTE SYSTEM

The Hindu social system, or caste system, is certainly not perfect but it establishes a coherent society allowing the coexistence of very different ways of life and beliefs. This system survived six centuries of difficult conditions: invasions, colonisations and then the establishment of democracy in modern India. Ancient texts—"laws of Manu"—set thes rules defining the duties and privileges of the various groups. Each one belongs to a caste, which constitutes a great family. Fortune does not enter in the relationship between the castes.

In Hinduism there are four castes arranged in a hierarchy. Anyone who does not belong to these castes is an outcast. The religious word for caste is "Varna". Each Varna has certain duties and rights. Each Varna member has to work in a certain trade, and only the members of that Varna are allowed to do these jobs. Each Varna has a defined diet. The highest Varna is the Brahmin. The members of this class are priests. The Varna below them in hierarchy is the Kshatriya. Its members are the warriors, the rulers of society and the aristocrats. Below them, the Vaishya's the farmers and the tradesmen. Then we have the Shudra's. Members of this caste are the craftsmen and the working class people who do the "non-polluting" type jobs. The caste hierarchy ends here. Below these castes are the outcasts who are the Untouchables for the four previous castes: they are called pariahs. "Pariah" means "drummer", a word of Portuguese origin derived from the Tamil word "paraḷ" (big drum). Being a drummer is an impure occupation because the skin of the drum comes from a dead animal. The Untouchables have degrading professions such as sewage jobs, cleaners, gravediggers, tanners, etc…

Each Varna—including the Untouchables—is divided into several communities. These communities are called Jats or Jātis. For example the Brahmins have Jāti called Gaur, Maithil, Sarjupari, Kankubja, Sarasvat, Iyer and others. People can only marry a member of the same Jāti. People are born within their Jāti and cannot change it.

The Portuguese, the first European power to arrive in India, distorted the word "Jāti" into caste. The British—who arrived in India much later—also used the word caste. Sometimes, in English, the word caste is used for Varna and the word sub-caste for Jāti.

All the Jātis accept that the Brahmin's Varna is the highest Varna in the hierarchy and that the Untouchables are the outcasts and belong to the lowest caste. But most of the Jātis in various Varnas claim to be superior and higher ranked than other Jātis. In most of the cases there is a connection between someone's profession and his Varna. In west India the oil-pressing Jātis is called Somwar Teli, the shepherds' Jāti is called Dhangar. And the Jāti of the cowherds is called Gaoli. The Kunbis's Jāti is the farmers. But some of the professions have different status in some parts of India and they are located at different levels within the caste hierarchy. For example the Dhobīs (washermen), are seen as the Untouchables in the North of India, whereas in the West of India they enjoy a Shudra status. The oil pressers in the East of India are seen as the Untouchables, whereas in central India they have a high status and in West India, a Shudra status.

There are also many cases where the Jāti members do not have the profession allocated to their Varna. Many Brahmins, who are supposed to be priests do not find jobs as priests or, do not manage to feed their families as priests, so they work as simple farmers. On the other hand there are many Brahmins who are landowners or tradesmen, i.e., professions supposedly belonging to the Vaishya Varna. The various Jāti members respect this rule most of the time and people who dare to breach it are outcast. As a rule, each community member only marries a member of their own community within their own Jāti.

Hinduism has many strict diet rules. The Brahmin Jāti have strict dietary habits. They will not eat in lower Jāti homes or even with lower Jāti (because of this, many restaurants hire Brahmin cooks). The Brahmin diet is supposed to include only vegetarian food. A Jāti who claims to have a higher Brahmin status also adopts the Brahmin's vegetarian diet. But there are some Brahmin Jātis that traditionally eat meat, fish, chicken and egg (which is considered non-vegetarian). Some Brahmin's in Kashmir, Orissa, Bengal and Mahārāshtra also eat meat. But this meat is never beef.

In the beginning the caste system was not a strict system and people could move from one Varna to another according to their Karma at the time. Indologists give various dates as to when this period of changes happened. Some claim that the change occurred around 500 B.C. and others date it about 500 A.D. Up until then, communities—or even a single person—could move from one Varna to another Varna, if they wanted to change jobs. There were some kings who belonged to the Kshatriya (warrior castes) who changed their status to become religious Brahmins. There were also those who changed their status to become warriors.

In the Indian society people who work in ignominious, polluting and unclean professions are seen as polluting people and are therefore considered as Untouchables. The Untouchables have almost no rights in society. In the several parts of India they are treated in diverse ways. In some regions the attitude towards the Untouchables was harsh and strict for example in Southern India they were expected to ring a bell like the lepers to announce their approach so that not even their shadows should fall on members of the higher castes. In other areas it was less strict.

In regions where the attitude was less strict, the Untouchables were seen as polluting people and their dwellings are situated at a certain distance from the settlements of the other four Varnas. The Untouchables are not allowed to touch people from these four Varnas. They were not allowed to enter their houses or even take water from the wells of the higher Varnas or even offer them water to drink. They were not allowed to enter the temples. At public events they were compelled to sit at a certain distance from the four other Varnas. In regions where the attitude towards the Untouchables was more severe, not only touching them is seen as polluting, but even having their shadow fall upon one was seen as polluting. According to orthodox rules anyone who did not belong to the four Varnas, i.e the foreigners, were Untouchables. Religiously anyone who did not belong to the four Varnas was an outcast and Untouchable. This means that all foreigners (mleccha) and non-Hindus are all supposed to be Untouchables. But in reality neither foreigners nor non-Hindus are treated as such these days.

Not every Indian resident is part of the caste system. About 7 % of India's population is referred to by their tribe and not by their caste or Jāti. They prefer to live away from society, and stay deep in the jungle, forests and mountains of India. They survive mostly on fishing, hunting or simple agriculture. These tribes have different religious beliefs and different gods. Some of them have simple beliefs, but others sacrifice human beings in their ceremonies. One such tribe, called Gond, has a strong kingdom in central India. Most of the tribes have adopted Hinduism, whilst others have adopted Islam or Christianity.

There are various theories about the establishment of the caste system. According to the Rig Veda, the ancient Hindu book, the primal man (Purush) destroyed himself to create a human society. The different Varnas were created from the parts of his body. The Brahmans were created from his head, the Kshatriya from his hands, the Vaishya from his thighs and the Shudras from his feet. Another religious theory claims that the Varnas were created from the body organs of Brahmā, who is the creator of the world.

The social historical theory explains the creation of the Varnas, the Jātis and the Untouchables. According to this theory, the caste system began with the arrival of the Aryans in India. The Aryans arrived in India around 1500 BC. They organised themselves in three groups and imposed a system of caste.

The colour of the skin was an important factor in the caste system. The meaning of the word "Varna" is not class or status, but skin colour.

As in most of the societies in the world—including India—the son inherits his father's profession. Thus families in India live according to their profession -one generation after the other i.e. the son keeps his father's profession. Later on, as these families become larger, they are seen as a community or Jāti, in the Indian language.

The leaders of independent India decided that India should be a democratic country. According to this policy, there is a separation between religion and state. Discrimination against the Untouchables or any person, based on his caste or creed, is legally prohibited. Along with this law, the government even allows positive discrimination (reservation of jobs and seats in schools of higher learning) towards the repressed castes of India.

Mahātma Gāndhi gave the Untouchables the name of Harijans (born of Hari, children of God). Indians have also become more flexible when it comes to their caste system customs. In general the urban people of India are less strict about the caste system than the rural ones.

PURE AND IMPURE

This opposition gives its coherence to the Hindu social system. It helps us to understand why the Brahmin is placed at the top of the scale, because what defines the Brahmin is absolute purity. The idea of purity relies on various criteria, and it is not simply the antithesis of impurity. The Brahmin must observe certain rules: the knowledge of divine, asceticism, refusal of violence, and vegetarianism…The society's ways are most importantly based on this "pure-impure" opposition. The pure one being incarnated in the body of a Brahmin and the impure one is represented by the lower castes. However, this concept is only put into perspective by the existence of subdivisions within the castes themselves. In each one of them, a special hierarchy is also set by on the level of superiority and purity. The religious values and the purity granted to some shall never match others. The scrupulous observance of the laws and duties of dharma, the pursuit of concrete interests (artha) and desire (kāma)—according to the god of Love—are the three human goals (purusārtha). These criteria follow a perfect hierarchy, albeit the aspiration for deliverance (moksha) is the supreme goal for everybody. The dharma is rather the Brahmans' objective, whereas the artha is more sought after by the people with power. But whatever the goal, the impure remains in a lower cast in relation Brahmans who represent the concept of purity.

SATĪ

Satī is described as a Hindu custom where the widow is burnt on the funeral pyre of her late husband. The Satī required this action to be voluntarily carried out so that the woman in her despair would decide to end her life after the death of her husband in order to remain faithful to him (Satī: act of faith). But in many cases, the women were forced to throw themselves to the flames. Sometimes they were even dragged to the lit pyre against their will.

Although Satī is considered a Hindu habit, the women, known under the name of Satī in the Hindu religious literature, did not inevitably commit suicide on their husbands' pyres. The first woman known under the Satī denomination was Shiva's wife. She threw herself into the fire to protest against her father, who had not shown to her husband, Shiva, all due respect. While burning, she requested to be reincarnated as Shiva's new wife. This is how she was to become Pārvatī.

These women who, in the Hindu mythology, symbolized the true Indian wife who devotes herself entirely to her husband, were called Satīs. But the custom to burn the widow on the dead husband's pyre does not find its origin or its justification in the religion.

There are various theories about the origins of the Satīs. One of them points out that Satīs prevented the wives from poisoning their rich husbands in order to marry their true lovers.

Although Satī is regarded as an Indian or a Hindu habit, it was not practised everywhere in India, not by all Hindus, but only in certain communities. On the other hand, the sacrifice of the widow on the pyre of her dead husband was not specific to India. It also happened within a lot of ancient communities. This habit was widespread among Egyptians, Greeks, Goths, and Scythes…Within these communities, they used to bury their dead kings with their mistresses, wives, or servants so that they could continue to serve them in the afterlife.

Another theory recounts that the Satī was probably imported to India by the Scythe invaders. When Scythes arrived in India, they adopted the Indian use of cremating the dead. And thus instead of burying their kings with their servants, they started to cremate their dead with their spouses.

Various Indian sovereigns tried to ban this habit. The Mughals tried to forbid it, but to no avail. The English prohibited it in 1829.

It is difficult to know with precision how many Satīs cases there have ever been. Before it got banned, there were a few hundred official cases each year. But, even after the prohibition, there were still some cases. It took a few decades before the custom disappeared. But some rare occurrences of Satīs remain nowadays. In 1987, with the blessing of the members of her family, an eighteen-years-old widow was the subject of a Satī ritual in the village of Rājasthān. In this particular case, the villagers took part in the ceremony, congratulated and supported the widow for her action. In October 1999, a woman hysterically jumped into her husband's pyre surprising everyone. But it was more likely an admitted suicide rather than a Satī case, because this woman was not obliged, neither forced nor even congratulated for her action.

In the different communities in India, Satī was practised for different reasons and in various ways. These Satīs were honoured and their families respected. It was believed that the woman who had carried out a Satī was blessing her family for seven generations. Religious temples were built to honour of the Satīs.

In certain communities where polygamy was authorized, only one wife was allowed to carry out a Satī. This wife was normally the preferred wife of the husband. It was a way of honouring this wife and the other wives considered it as a kind of dishonour. In other communities, one or more wives or mistresses were immolated with their husbands, as were certain male servants with the kings. This kind of Satī where the wives and the servants were treated as objects supports the theory that Satī was imported into India by the Scythe invaders. In some very rare cases, the mothers made Satī on their sons' pyres and in much rarer cases the husbands carried out Satī on their wives' pyres. This practice was prohibited in 1829, but had to be banned again in 1956 following the reoccurrence of some cases. Another resurgence of this practice took place in 1981 and one new provision in 1987 tried to stop its propagation. The Satī justifies the idea that women are not worth much compared to men.

INTERVIEWS WITH LOCAL RESIDENTS

Where to get the best information on Kāshī, if not from its population, i.e. the actors and the heart and soul of this town full of mysteries? This is why, it seemed important for us to hand over to them.

DOM FAMILY: Manikarnikā ghāt, burning ghāt

6th December 2004 in the morning:

Manikarnikā ghat is the main and most popular cremation ground in Kāshī, where funeral pyres burn all day and all night. They are owned by the Dom families, or "The Untouchables" (touching the dead is considered to be impure, so cremation is only practised by the low castes). They have been, through generations, the guardians of the sacred fire—for thousands of years. Each year

there are more than 30,000 cremations in Kāshī, 28,000 in Manikarnikā alone. Hindus believe that those who die and are cremated here, in Kāshī, get an instant gateway to liberation from the cycle of births and re-births. For it is supposed that here the Lord Shiva in the form of Tarakeshwar whispers the Moksha Mantra into the ears of all the departed souls that arrive there. This is what they call Moksha.

Poetry painted on the white washed wall above the ghāt of Manikarnikā

This is Manikarnikā, where death is auspicious
Where life is fruitful
Where one grazes the pastures of heaven.
There is no tīrtha like Manikarnika
There is no city like Kāshī,
There is no linga like Vishveshvara,
Not in the whole universe.

Question   : What are your names?
Dom Family : Badrilal Choudhury
               Raj Kumar Choudhury.
Question   : How old are you?
Dom Family : I am 60 years old.
               And me, I am around 40 years old.
Question   : Were you born in Vārānasī?
Dom Family : Of course, I was born in Kāshī. I prefer
               to say Kāshī because it is the name of
               our city of light, this is its original name
               and the most beautiful one. We are from
               the Dom family. Our family works in the
               two burning ghāts, called Manikarnikā
               ghāt and Harishandra ghāt. We are
               descendants of Kalu Dom. I am the boss
               of the two sites. Nobody can be burned
               here without my permission. But I have
               a big family.
Question   : Since when does the Dom family work
               in the burning ghāts?
Dom Family : All my family has been working at this
               job for several thousands of years.
               Our job is to provide the sacred fire
               necessary to all the cremations. Lord

Shiva created this place called Mani-
karnikā and it is the most important place.
Question   : Is there any competition between the two
               ghāts?
Dom Family : For the "Moksha", (the liberation of the
               cycle of reincarnation), it's better to be
               burnt in the Manikarnikā ghāt. But
               everybody who is burnt in Kāshī will
               get Moksha—but the best place is in
               Manikarnikā.
Question   : What is the importance of the holy fire?
Dom Family : This fire is like a god. For that reason
               we care for it with a lot of attention. We
                are the guard-ians of this fire.
               After having turned five times
               around the dead body saying
               the names of the gods, the son
               of the family applies the holy
               fire, and lights the fire, starting
               at the mouth of the dead.
Question   : How do you look after this fire?
Dom Family : At all time, day and night somebody is
               supervising the fire so that it does not
               die. It has been burning for several
               thousands of years. It has never died.
Question   : Even during the monsoon , during
               invasions, wars…? ?
Dom Family : Never, never…
Question   : What are, step by step, the process of a
               cremation?
Dom Family : The dream of every Hindu is to be
               burned in Kāshī to obtain Moksha. So

many families come with the body of the dead to be cremated here or people come here before they die to be sure they will get burned in this place. Many, many people are waiting for their death here in Kāshī. It is very important in our religion. Families come to Manikarnikā carrying the dead body on a bamboo stretcher chanting prayers. When they arrive at the burning ghāt, they deposit the body near the water on the bank, and present it in front of Gangā after immersing it into the river. Each member of the family fills the mouth of the dead with the water of Gangā. Then they cover the body with different things like vermilion powder, incense…They shave their hair and they get dressed in white clothes. Then they ask our family for the fire—the holy fire. They pay for that—without payment, fire is not given. The cost is not the same for everybody. It depends whether they have a lot of money or whether they are poor people. After that, they come back to the body which is laid down on the pyre. The oldest son turns five times around the pyre and lights the body starting by the mouth.

Question : How much is the price for a cremation?

Dom Family : It depends on the people; it depends on the wood, if there is a lot of wood and also what kind of wood is used. There is not a fixed price. Cremating a dead body consumes, on average, about 500 kg of wood.

Question : What happens when poor people cannot pay the price?

Dom Family : There is always somebody there to pay the price or to help the family.

Question : Some people are directly pushed into the Gangā without being burned? Why?

Dom Family : If it is a holy man (sādhu), a pregnant woman, a baby, somebody killed by a snake's bite or in some other cases, it is allowed by the religion to put their body into Gangā without cremation, because they are already pure.

Question : Have you seen some cases of Sati, here in Kāshī? (Authors note: Sati is a Hindu custom in India whereby widows are burnt to death on their husband's pyre. It can also be by personal choice or forced upon the women by her in-laws. This custom was prohibited in 1829.)

Dom Family : Never. Now the Sati tradition is finished. It is not allowed. There are some cases in the countryside, but they are very rare. I have never seen that here in Kāshī.

Question : In Manikarnikā, there is a special site for Sati; can you talk about that particular place?

Dom Family : Just down there, there is a place where Sati was practised in the past. It is the temple of Sati. People pray to them like Gods.

Question : Where do the names of Manikarnikā and Harischandra ghāts come from?

Dom Family : King Harischandra worked in this burning ghat for twelve months, but it is a very long story. And the name of Manikarnikā has several origins. Some say that Shiva shivered in delight when he saw what Vishnu had created, dropping an earring into the pool, others say that it was the earring of Satī, Shiva's dead wife, hence the name Manikarnikā: "jewelled earring".

Question : What is the sense of a cremation here in Kāshī for a Hindu?

Dom Family : Only Hindu people want to be burned in Kāshī. It represents the most important purification and, especially, Moksha, the end of reincarnation, like paradise for the Catholics, or Nirvana for the Buddhists.

Question : How long does a cremation take?

Dom Family : Around three hours. It depends on the body, if it is a man, a woman or a child or if there is a lot of wood or not.

Question : Do women come to the cremation ceremony?

Dom Famil : Yes, it is possible. (Author's note: women very rarely attend)

Question : Sometimes dogs come to the cremation ghāt. Why? Is that not a bit shocking?

Dom Family : They don't eat the remains of the body; they are just attracted by the smell.

Question : In Western countries, when somebody dies, people cry. Here in India, it is not the case, although I am sure they are sad. Why?

Dom Family : Most of the time, they cry at home, in the street when they are coming with the body, but when they arrive here, they realise that there is no death, only Moksha. It is our deliverance, our liberation.

Question : What is the meaning of Ma Gangā?

Dom Family : Like the Gangā, that never stops flowing, here in Kāshī people never die because, with Moksha, they can enter into eternity. Moksha cuts the cycle of birth and death, it stops the cycle of reincarnation. People become like Gangā, like the holy fire, they never die. That is the kind of feeling we have, a feeling of eternity, especially here in Manikarnikā.

PILGRIMS

Kāshī is the city of pilgrimage par excellence. This pilgrimage is itself worth all of the other pilgrimages put together. Being a town of devotions and perpetual dialogue with the Gods, throughout the year, millions of pilgrims from all over India gather in front of the jyotirlingam (lingam of light) of the Vishvanāth temple—and in front of Gangā's holy water. There are five holy roads in Kāshī, five routes of pilgrimage (Chaurashikroshī,

Panchakroshī, Nagar Pradakshinā, Avimukta, Antargriha vis. Rana P B Singh *Banaras Region: A Spiritual and Cultural Guide*). Whether you come from a small village or a megalopolis, the feeling of fervour remains the same. Sneha Dasgupta, an English teacher in Kolkata and her daughter, Shyamali, came as well to meet the gods.

29th December 2004: Dashāsvamedh ghāt

Question : What are your names?
Pilgrims : Our names are Sneha and Shyamali Dasgupta.
Question : How old are you?
Pilgrim : I am forty-two and my daughter is fourteen years old.
Question : Where are you coming from?
Pilgrim : We are from Kolkata. West Bengal.
Question : How did you come to Kāshī?
Pilgrim : We came by train.
Question : What are the reasons of your journey?
Pilgrim : The first reason is pilgrimage, and also to visit Kāshī, the holy temples, especially Vishvanāth Mandir (temple), Annapūrnā Bhavānī Mandir (temple), Nepali Mandir (temple) and also many other ones. We have to go inside barefoot. It is a way to show our respect to the Gods.
Question : What is the most important temple of the city?
Pilgrim : Vishvanāth temple is very, very important, the most important. Very important for all Hindus. All Hindus want to pray to the Shiva lingam of the Vishvanāth temple. It is very sacred. Vishvanāth and Annapūrnā Bhavānī are both other names for Shiva. Annapūrnā is a goddess who gives wealth, money, and food…
Question : Is this your first pilgrimage to Kāshī?
Pilgrim : This is my third pilgrimage to Kāshī. Every year I try to come here, because this pilgrimage is very important for me. It is like a purification. Last night I was at the pūjā here in Dashāsvamedh, and when I participated in this pūjā I was really happy. I want to return today. The feeling I can have there is very impressive. If I want to obtain some things, that is also a good way. I was walking to many ghāts: Asi ghāt, Mīr ghāt, Dashāsvamedh ghāt, Manikarnikā and Harischandra ghāts, and Kedāra ghāt. I took holy dips; I took some holy water to bring home. I will take back many sweets, "prasād," offered to the gods, to give to my family and friends. I took photos of Vishvanāth.

Question	: Do you think that your pilgrimage contribute to your wealth, your happiness?
Pilgrim	: Of course. Since I have been coming here to Kāshī, I am like everybody…I have ups and downs in my life but it's a gain. My life is better. For my daughter, it is the same. Every year, she insists in coming with me. Each year she is doing better and better in her studies. And I hope she'll become a doctor as she wishes.
The daughter	: Kāshī is my lucky place. And later on I want to do my studies here in the BHU, the Banāras Hindus University. I think my studies get better and better because I come every year to Kāshī, it contributes to it.
Question	: Do you think that this pilgrimage is also very fruitful for your Karma?
Pilgrim	: Yes, certainly. If I am lucky enough to be burnt here in Manikarnikā, I will go straight away to heaven. I don't know what is heaven, maybe it is a feeling. But I am waiting for Moksha. I want to be burnt in Manikarnikā, that is my best wish. After a pilgrimage, I feel mentally better, I feel happiness. I have the real feeling of a purification of my mind and my body, both of them together. I feel powerful, peaceful. I feel new, regenerated.
Question	: Are there some other places of pilgrimage as important in India?
Pilgrim	: Yes of course there are several thousand

places of pilgrimage, like in the Himalayas Gangotrī, Kedārnāth Yamunotrī, Gaumukh, Badrīnāth.

Question	: What is in your view, the value of a Pilgrimage in Kāshī?
Pilgrim	: The River Gangā is here. It is very important. The River Gangā is like our Mother. It also flows through Kolkata. But it is very important here also because there are thousands of Shiva Lingam here. It is very powerful…If somebody has only one pilgrimage to do in his life it must be to Kāshī.
Question	: What is the meaning of Gangā for you?
Pilgrim	: Wherever Gangā flows, the river gives prosperity, it gives fish to the people, food and provides wealth to the boatmen. And it is also a very beautiful river and a very powerful river.
Question	: Where are the main points where the pilgrims have to stop on their way?
Pilgrim	: We call these places "tīrtha". There are five tīrthas here in Kāshī: Asi ghāt, Manikarnikā, Dashāsvamedh, Panchagangā ghāt, Ādi Keshava ghāt. Many pilgrims do the journey barefoot. Some others go by boat. Sometimes I go by boat, sometimes, I walk.
Question	: How long are you staying here?
Pilgrim	: I have been here for four days but we have to leave today. We feel very sad to go back.

Question	: If you should have to choose a place to die, which place would it be?
Pilgrim	: Of course it would be Kāshī. If I die in Kolkata, it is impossible for me to be burnt in Manikarnikā. It is not possible. It is for that reason that people come here to die.
Question	: Have you made other Pilgrimages in other parts of India?
Pilgrim	: I have been to Badrīnāth, Gangotrī, Yamunotrī, Purī, and Kalighāt in Bengal. But Kāshī is all year long in my mind. Here there is a very special feeling.

SĀDHU:

Shibananda is a sādhu. There are several brotherhoods of sādhus. He belongs to the Rāmānandis. It was set up in compliance with the teachings of Rāmānanda, a philosopher who lived in Kāshī during the 15th century. The followers are also called Vairāgī, those who are indifferent to the world, and Avadhūta, those who gave up everything. His deep blue eyes glance at you with a rare gentleness. And his kindness towards people is as gentle as his wit.

Question	: What is your name?
Shibananda	: My name is Shibananda.
Question	: Can I ask you how old you are?
Shibananda	: I do not know my age and I do not have any ID to prove it to you.
Question	: You really don't have any idea about it?
Shibananda	: It's not necessary.
Question	: So then, can we say that you are very young?
Shibananda	: Maybe…I don't know my age whatsoever.
Question	: Where were you born?
Shibananda	: I was born in Bengal, in a small village close to Bolpur.
Question	: What kind of family do you come from?
Shibananda	: A normal family. Totally normal.
Question	: How old were you when you started to be a sādhu?
Shibananda	: Oh, that was a very long time ago. I've travelled for more than 30 years.
Question	: How old were you when you started to travel?
Shibananda	: I was very young when I began my travels. Maybe in my twenties, maybe less.
Question	: How does the idea of becoming a sādhu come to the mind of a young man?
Shibananda	: At that time, I had very good friends. They introduced me to a group. I met there my guru, my Master in religion. And I was very impressed by this person. I stayed with him for a long time. I learned very much with him.
Question	: Was he also a Baba (an affectionate name given to the sādhus)?
Shibananda	: Yes, of course.

Question : Before you met him, did you have a religious spirit? Were you interested in it?

Shibananda : Since my childhood, I felt religious and I was attracted by these kind of things. But I was very lucky to meet this guru.

Question : How can you become a sādhu?

Shibananda : Everyone can be a sādhu. If somebody wishes to live this kind of life, he can do it.

Question : Can you speak to me about this life?

Shibananda : We have no family, no home, we have nothing, absolutely nothing. People have a house, a family, children…We do not have anything at all.

Question : How many hours of meditation do you do each day?

Shibananda : Two hours, sometimes three hours. The older I get, the more I sit to meditate.

Question : Do you practise yoga?

Shibananda : I practise yoga, but it is not the most important thing for me, I prefer meditation.

Question : Are all sādhus regarded as gurus?

Shibananda : Yes, in general. In the Indian system, everything is based on a system of knowledge exchange. I've learned things, so it's now my turn to teach. I was once a disciple, and then it was my turn to have disciples who came to me. Step by step, one progresses towards knowledge. I explain how to do that, which way to take, there are so many ways…there are so many different ways to see the same things, whether you are Hindu, Muslim, Catholic, Protestant…Some people see things only through Rāma, others through Shiva or Krishna…

Question : Do you teach sacred texts from the Mahābhārata, the Vedas, the Bhagavad-Gītā or from other ones?

Shibananda : Yes, there are books for absolutely everyone. They are very important books. But there are various ways to reach knowledge. Religion is like a house, you can come from the east, the west, the south or the north, you can come from everywhere. The house is there, and we all meet everyone in that very house and go inside it. The meeting point is the same one. It is like water, it can freeze and become an ice cube, it has a shape, and then melts and has no shape anymore. As for the mind, it is the same thing. We can believe in the shape, in the matter, or not believe in it. It is like God. We believe in God or we do not believe in it. Who is God? We don't know who is God. What shape has he got? Maybe he is male or female. Nobody knows it. Some people call it Allah others call it God. If somebody says: "no, it is not him!" Who is right? The names are different, but the essence is the same. It is like when you wear a shirt and then you change it. The

191

envelope is different but the person inside it is the same one. When we are born, we don't have a name or a religion. Nothing. The parents are the ones who give us a religion "You must go to church". "No, no, you must go to the temple…" "To the mosque…" We are born absolutely naked.

Question : Is it for this reason that the sādhus do not own anything? Some of them, the nagas, even live totally naked?

Shibananda : We don't know when we will leave. Material things don't help us. When we are born, we do not have anything and when we die, we will take nothing with us. What 's the point in owning anything in between these two periods? It is a rotation.

Question : Is it difficult to live as a renunciate?

Shibananda : What will be the use for me of having a beautiful house, a beautiful car, of having money, and thinking all the time about money? One day you go away and you leave everything behind you.

Question : What do you live on?

Shibananda : I don't need anything. I live very simply. I don't need a large bag a small one is enough.

Question : Are we in your home? Where are we?

Shibananda : I am in this house. Somebody lends me this small room to sleep. I just pass.

Question : Are all your belongings in this bedroom?

Shibananda : Yes. There is a lingam, a trident (trishūl), a Nandī statue (a bull, which is the vehicle of Shiva and is adored as such. It symbolizes justice and rectitude), some flowers, some books, no clothes, no futile objects. Maybe I will be reincarnated as an animal, as a tree…

Question : How important is yoga?

Shibananda : Above all, yoga is a series of physical exercises to control the body. To control the mind, meditation is more advisable.

Question : What does Kāshī represent for you? Is it a special city?

Shibananda : Yes, of course it is a special city. We call it the town of Shiva. Everyone knows this city. Really, this city has a special meaning. Nobody knows since when it exists, but it is certainly the oldest inhabited city in all the history of humanity.

Question : Have you been living in Kāshī for a long time?

Shibananda : No. Before I used to come and go. I used to never stay here. I came and went along all the roads, everywhere in India, in Nepal.

Question : How long have you been living in Kāshī?

Shibananda : Two or three years ago, a family offered me to settle here. It is quite recent.

Question : As the years go by, do you think that Kāshī has changed a lot?

Shibananda : Yes, very much. It is nowadays a touristic place and that has changed the landscape.

It is like Rājasthān, now it's nonsense…A lot of pollution…

Question : So do you think that Kāshī is becoming like Rājasthān?

Shibananda : No, but I don't know for how long we will be able to control the situation. But gradually it is becoming a touristic place.

Question : Do you think that the spirituality of Kāshī is disappearing because of this tourist phenomenon?

Shibananda : No, it cannot disappear, because this city is connected to its river. Gangā is so sacred, so important here. There are so many temples…Everything is built around the river, around these temples. We have an immense respect for this river.

Question : Do you think that Kāshī can lose its soul?

Shibananda : No, I do not believe it.

Question : How could materialism, modernism be a danger to Hinduism, or to Kāshī?

Shibananda : Today young people want to be modern. They follow the tourists. Sometimes, they even change their first names into western names. They want to immitate Westerners. They don't want to go to school anymore. They speak English very well but if you ask them to write something, that's impossible.

Question : Does Kāshī lose something because of this modernity?

Shibananda : In a way Kāshī is damaging itself.

Question : Many sādhus use drugs. Do you? What do you think about it?

Shibananda : It is a big question. Many people use them but I am not interested in that.

Question : Not even a small chilum sometimes?

Shibananda : No, never.

Question : No ganja, no hashish?

Shibananda : Never. I never touched that.

Question : But do the other sādhus often smoke a lot of of ganja?

Shibananda : They like it and smoke very much. Me, I don't like that. Shiva never said that you have to smoke the chilum.

Question : Do You know Karl Marx?

Shibananda : Yes, of course.

Question : Karl Marx said that religion was the "opium of the people". What do you think about this way of thinking with regards to India, which is a country where religion has a great importance?

Shibananda : All the religions are made by men and not by the Gods. All the temples, all the churches or the mosques were built by men and not by the Gods. People enter them and worship. Religions are used to control society. All the religions give instructions on how to behave, on what to do, or not do. It is necessary to control the human activity, the mental activity. Without these marks, men could lose themselves. Men are afraid of religion. So religions are necessary.

Question : Is this just a way to live or is it rather a way of not being subversive against society?

Shibananda : All religions have a power over people. But men are the most beautiful creation of the Gods. Religions are like the roots of life.

Question : What do you think about the caste system? Is this also a way of controlling people?

Shibananda : It is a very old system, which has existed for thousands of years. Not everyone can have the same profession, the castes compartmentalize human activities, thus the barbers remain with barbers, the milkmen with the milkmen, the priests remain with their sacred activities. And you have to marry and start a family within the same caste. It is a bit like in the army. There are several divisions and each one plays their own role.

Question : Is this a way of putting society in order?

Shibananda : This system is losing its strength. People do not work necessarily in their caste anymore. On the ghāts, we can see graffities that blame this system. Things will evolve but very slowly. Maybe India is not mature enough in its social structure and its old roots are so deeply anchored that it will be long and difficult to give up this ancestral order, which has been governing the society for millenniums.

Question : How do you imagine the future of India?

Shibananda : I don't know. Who knows?

Question : For you what is the meaning of life?

Shibananda : Life: vast subject. It depends on what you like. You choose your life. What do you really want to do? One person will be interested in politics, another one in religion, another one in nature, art, and sciences…To have the choice, to keep this choice and to know what you really like, what you want. Each person has his or her own way. The meaning of life is to go towards happiness. Happiness is the most important thing in life. I like this word.

साक्षात् शिव स्वरूप तैलंग स्वामी के साथ रामकृष्ण परमहंस ।

WIDOW

Kāshī is a city that attracts widows from all over India because it is their last refuge. In the month of Kārttika (November), to honour their husbands, they light up small lamps in wicker baskets, which are held on top of bamboo poles. These lamps light up the sky with a sad gleam.

Sometimes they live in houses reserved to them: the vidhwa ashrams. In the ancient tradition, women did not have the right to outlive their husbands. They had to immolate themselves on the husband's pyre. This practice called "Satī" was prohibited during the British rule in 1829. Even nowadays, they are rejected by their family-in-law, by their own family.

They have no resources and still have to bear a reputation of bringing bad luck. The Indian widow dresses in white, wanders in the lanes and on the ghāts waiting for their future liberation (moksha). An Indian

saying tells that there are four dangers to avoid in Kāshī: widows, bulls, stairs, and holy men. In India, less than 10% of the sādhus are women, most of them are widows rejected by everybody. Minakshi is one of these "sadhvi".

Question   : What is your name?
The Widow : My name is Minakshi Devī.
Question   : How old are you?
The Widow : I am 53 years old.
Question   : Where were you born?
The Widow : I was born in a small village in Bengal, not in Kāshī.

Question   : Can you tell us some episodes of your life?
The Widow : I was living happily in my village in Bengal, but at 17 years old, my family married me to a man. He was only a few years older than me—not very old. I only met him on the day of my marriage, as it is often the case in India. My parents had chosen my husband and I followed him to his family's home in the South of India. We were living happily. He was a good husband. He was a good workingman and looked after me well. But he died from illness seven years after our marriage. We did not have any child. No son, no girl. When he died, it was very hard for me. I found myself alone, I was a widow and I was only twenty-four years old. I was not working, and needed to earn money for a living. I worked hard. I was very sad, and because it was too difficult, I returned to my family. His family did not want to look after me. So I went back to Bengal. At first, it was fine. I was glad to see my family again. I liked them very much. But little by little, I felt that I had become a burden to them. They made me work. It was normal, and I wanted to be useful. But as time went by, they started to ask me to work more and more. From very early in the morning until very late in the evening. All day long, I was doing the work that the others did

not want to do. I did not rebel. I did my work. But they started to become nasty with me, they started to beat me, it became humiliating. I was very badly treated. They never looked after me. My own parents had rejected me. My family made me feel that I was a burden to them. I had left home with my husband and now, I was back to my family, but I did not have a place there anymore. They made me pay for it. I was very sad really. Then, one day, I could not stand this anymore, and I swallowed some poison. I almost died it was very painful. I wanted to die. Life had become too difficult for me, but I was very religious. As Hindu people, we are not allowed to commit suicide, and it was a very difficult decision to make. But despite the poison I did not die. I suffered a lot, but I survived. It was very hard for me to live after having done that. It was impossible to stay anymore. I was obliged to leave my family's house. They did not throw me out, but I felt that they would be relieved. When I left, I had absolutely nothing. I knew that I had to go to Kāshī. It is the only place where a widow can go. There are many widows in Kāshī. I never saw my family again.

Question   : Why do many widows come to Kāshī?
The Widow : Because here, we can wait for death, quietly. We know that if we die here, we will get the liberation (moksha), the end of the rebirths cycle. It is the only important thing when nothing else is left to a widow she is rejected by everybody. Kāshī is a special place where people come for pilgrimage. And if you want to obtain some merits that are good for your Karma, you have to help people like beggars. Some widows have absolutely nothing to live on. Begging can be a source of income. Sometimes, widows get together in vidhwa ashrams, waiting for their death. There are many widows in Kāshī. But the main reason for coming here, as for me, is to obtain the moksha, the ultimate deliverance. Kāshī is the only place in the world where you can get the moksha. But it is the same for everybody, not only for widows. For that reason, I want to stay in Kāshī.

Question   : What is your income?
The Widow : I have a very small pension paid by the Indian State. But that is not enough to live on. A brother of mine sends me a little bit of money when he can, but it is rare. So, I live with almost nothing, I live very simply and spend my money only for food and for my rent. But I eat very little.

Question   : Why are you dressed in orange clothes and not in white clothes like the other widows?

The Widow: I am dressed in orange colour because I became Sannyāsin. It means that I gave up all the materialistic things, and I devote myself to praying. I pray all day long. You can see here, on the walls, there are only posters of Gods: Shiva, Ganesh, Pārvatī, Hanumān, we call that: mūrti. They protect me. I am for all the religions, it is very important to believe in Gods. Generally in India, widows are dressed in white, and they don't have the red mark in the hair anymore. That's how they are recognised. But me, I am dressed with orange colour, because I gave up everything. I go to an āshram and I pray with other sādhus. When I don't have enough money to pay the rent of my very small room, I go to this āshram to live with the other sādhus.

Question: Life for the widows in India is very, very difficult. Do you think that it can push a woman to commit suicide, by making her life impossible? Can it be seen as a form of modern Satī? (Satī is a Hindu practice in India. Widows would throw themselves in their husband's pyre, voluntarily or be pushed by their family-in-law. It was banned in 1829 by the English).

The Widow: It was my own choice to commit suicide. But I knew that my presence was not wished any more. And for an Indian widow, there are not many choices. It is as if we are already dead. Yes, I think that to make people feel so unhappy and to push them to commit suicide, is a kind of Satī. I would have liked to live because I was still very young. But after my husband's death, it was like I had lost my own existence. Everyday I pray the Gods, asking them to come to me. Everyday I go to the Kedāra Temple, even if I am ill (This is a temple visited by people from the South of India). People who commit suicide don't go to heaven. The body is like a temple. Everybody has a soul within. That is why we take care of our Karma. Everybody wants to go to heaven. With a suicide, it's impossible. But very often, the family-in-law makes life very hard for the widow, and even if she has children it becomes unbearable.

Question: People say that widows bring bad luck. It's like crossing a black cat? Do you have this feeling?

The Widow: Many people think exactly like that. Still now. It is an old tradition. People do not want to cross the road, to cross my way. It is the same thing when someone sneezes in the morning. Sneezing once brings bad luck. Twice, there is no problem. People believe in things like that.

Question: What are you waiting for in your future?

The Widow: I have not been waiting for anything for a long time. I am just waiting for my death. And I want to die here in Kāshī. It is the most important thing for me: to know that I will die here and pray the Gods unceasingly.

THE ROLE OF WOMEN IN INDIA

INTERVIEW WITH POONAM CHAWLA.

In India, most young girls are trained at home by their mothers for the most important day of their life: the marriage, the moment when they become real women. For more than 2000 years, the Hindu society has been structured by the laws of Manu that states that women: "depend on men, first of all her father, then her husband, and after his death, her son".

The birth of a girl is not as desirable as the birth of a boy because a dowry will have to be paid at the time of the marriage, this can sometimes amount to very high sums of money. Although the law has banned this practice since 1961, a dowry is almost always required by the boys family. The married woman is first subjected to the authority of her parents-in-law and then of her husband. Many reports reveal that violence towards women is increasing. The murders of brides  for insufficient dowry are frequent but the number of reported cases is increasing. It is thought that, each year in India more than 7,000 women are burned alive in cleverly made up scenarios due to unpaid dowries.

In the last twenty years, feminist movements have emerged and the women' status has improved. Nowadays, some women have got job positions traditionally taken by men and hence, they have got some independence. Here is the testimony of one of these women: Poonam Chawla.

Question	: What is your name?
Poonam	: My name is Poonam Chawla, my nationality is Indian and I live in Paris in France. I left India fourteen years ago. I was born in Pune, not very far from Bombay, but I spent most of my life in Delhi. I did all my studies in Delhi in a very dynamic University, the Jawaharlal Nehru University (JNU). I am 47 years old. I was married in India and I had two sons who were born from this marriage. When I got married, most of my friends had arranged marriages. At that time, when I married in 1982, there were not a lot of love marriages. I met my husband at the University. He fell in love with me, and I decided to say yes because I was afraid of an arranged marriage. Because I knew him and his family, I preferred to get married with him rather than with an unknown man. It was not the marriage wanted by my family. He was not of the same caste, and comes from Bengal. And this union was not at all envisaged or planned by them. It was very difficult for my family to accept the fact and though they could not do so from the heart they had to comply. India is a big country and my story is not really representative, but I belong to India even if I do not live there anymore. In India most marriages are arranged but you can find couples who

married for love, especially in the cities. It is really difficult to say what is the ratio of arranged marriages to love matches in India.

Question : Is an arranged marriage always programmed?

Poonam : Most of the time, marriages are arranged by the families. They are done through relationships, small ads or intermediaries. They are often decided according to astrological criteria. I have other friends who were not in this university. They had arranged marriages that worked out very well. Girls who married with a NRI (non resident Indian)—this happens often. They are Indians who live outside of India. At that time, many Indian girls wished to marry men who lived in a foreign country. But at times there were some marriages that in fact were false marriages, because these men were already married. Sometimes they agreed to marry because they did not dare to disagree with their parents, and/or they did not dare to tell them that they were already married abroad with a foreign woman. It was also a way to take the dowry. And when the young Indian woman came to settle down in the new home abroad, she realised that there was another woman. These cases are not very rare. I knew of such a case in my family.

Question : What do you think about the role and the place of the woman in India?

Poonam : The role of the woman in India is varied. It depends on the social background, the place, i.e., if she lives in the countryside or downtown. That depends on many factors. If she has money, it is good for her. If she has money, she has power.

Question : You say safety, meaning that they are easily attacked physically?

Poonam : Yes of course physically. But also in a more alienating way: through harassment. For example when I was younger, it started at the age of 12-13 years old; the boys in the streets, in the buses, harassed us. All the women who lived in the big cities had experiences like these, a little unpleasant. It can go up to sexual attacks, even rape. To keep safe, girls stay among themselves and do not accept the presence of boys. This is why girls always remain in groups. Meeting anybody of the opposite sex is not allowed in India. It is not proper to stay with men, and it is one of the reasons why boys are frustrated. And sometimes this kind of frustrations leads the men to excesses. The bonds between men and women happen most of the time only through relationships in the marriage or through the family relationships. For example, when somebody came at home and knocked on the door, it was always my father who opened the door. It was never my mother or myself who would open the door.

Question : Is it possible to think that with time, Indian women will find their place, or is it still difficult for them to be controlled by her father or her husband?

Poonam : Women find their place gradually. We find this phenomenon especially in the cities, because in the villages or the small cities her status is still that of submission. In the big cities the women become increasingly independent and their place becomes more comfortable.

Question : So socially it is only in the cities that their condition is improving, is that true also with regards to their family status?

Poonam : That really depends on the families. In the very traditional families the women do not have a true place yet.

Question : Tell us about the dowry. Although this practice is illegal, it is still very common.

Poonam : In fact, we cannot say that the dowry is really abolished. I had a dowry. Everybody has a dowry. I spoke yesterday with my sister in law who lives in Delhi who told me about a marriage she was invited to, which had been cancelled because the family of the husband asked for a more expensive dowry than the one that had been agreed previously. There are arrangements before the marriage. When the woman is definitely married, she leaves her own family, and she takes the entire dowry for the in-law family. Part of it can be paid a few days before the marriage.

Question : Can you tell us about the problems involved with the dowry and the "accidents in the home" which are the consequences of the dowry?

Poonam : Usually these problems take place in families that are not very rich. Normally the dowry is assessed according to the families' wealth. So when there are specific requests all the problems begin. Because what happens is that the families always want more than what has been negotiated.

Question : Is there a written contract for the dowry?

Poonam : No, absolutely not. There are always verbal and/or implied agreements.

Question : Tell us about the role of the family-in-law in a couple's life.

Poonam : The family-in-law is very important because it is the family-in-law who replaces the bride's family. It also depends whether the couple lives with the family or lives independently. But in all cases, the family-in-law retains a major role. But it is however very common that, even in big cities, couples live with the husband's parents. It is the traditional rule. It entails problems as regards to the lack of intimacy. Sometimes this situation can be difficult to live with. Often people are very stressed by this lack of privacy. In the Occident, there is the stress to live alone—in India it is rather the opposite.

Question : Is it still common that the husband and wife only meet on their wedding's day?

Poonam : It still happens, of course, in the countryside or in the small cities, but it is becoming rare in the big towns. The future-married couples meet two-three or four times before they decided to get married. But often there are marriages where the couples meet only once. It is the most common practice. When my parents got married, they had never met before.

Question : What happens to the woman on the death of her husband?

Poonam : That depends a lot on the situation. It is very difficult to generalize. I lost my brother when I was very young. He only died ten months after his marriage. His wife decided to stay with us. But such a situation is very rare. Usually, it depends on many criteria like the duration of the marriage, if there were children or not, if it is a rich or educated family. Sometimes if the marriage did not last long and that there were no children, the widow returns to her parents' who will try to marry her again. But sometimes, in the villages, she is rejected. Traditionally within low educated circles, she has the reputation of bringing bad luck.

Question : The role of a good Hindu is to give a son to the descendants. What happens when the couple cannot have children or when one of them is sterile?

Poonam : When the woman is sterile, sometimes it is accepted for the husband to bring a new wife to his home. For a Hindu family, the son is really very important because the girl is very expensive due to the dowry that will have to be paid for her future wedding. So families prefer to have boys. And then the parents get a sort of old-age pension, because they stay with their son when they become older. In the North of India, back home in the Punjāb region, parents stay with their son. When parents pay a visit to their daughter, they usually pay for their stay because according to practice they do not eat or take anything at their daughter's house. That happens in the North of India especially. When my mother comes to see me, she calculates the expenditure and gives me a certain sum. My brother, on the other hand, pays a kind of pocket money to my mother.

Question : Talk to us about the so-called women victims of accidents in the home?

Poonam : It is difficult to speak about it. When I lived in India, everyday there were two or three cases reported in the newspapers.

They were acknowledged as accidents in the home. But we knew very well that it was not true. Often people joked about it, by saying that it only occurred on Sunday evenings, because, indeed, every Sunday evening everyone watched a big movie on television. At that time, twenty years ago, there were not as many programmes as there are today, and everybody watched the Sunday evening feature movie. And these so-called accidents took place only at that time, when people were glued to their television sets. Nobody heard the shouts. But I personally never had any direct link with such a situation. In India, we still use small kerosene stoves. To sprinkle kerosene on women was an easy way to pretend it was an accident and not a murder.

Question : How do you explain that the number of men is higher than women in India?

Poonam : About thirty years ago when they discovered that it was possible to know the sex of a baby, there were private clinics everywhere who performed these ultrasound scans and as soon as the sex of the child was known, if it was female, it was easy to abort. In the south of India and in some areas, sometimes people poisoned small girls by making them swallow a few toxic seeds. This must still be happening in countryside areas of India or in deprived circles. An Indian director made a film in which he talks about the life of a village deprived of girls because they had all been aborted. Young men of twenty to twenty-five years old found themselves with no women around. This film is of course based on real facts.

Question : Nowadays is the system of the castes still significant?

Poonam : In the cities its significance is much lower than in the countryside or in remote areas. In the cities, one does not know whether one is sitting beside an untouchable and it does not matter. But in the villages this is not yet the case. Today, in cities like Delhi, money and power are notions that have taken over traditional practices. Differences among people are not only centred on the castes but also around the social and cultural background, the language and the area of origin.

Question : What pushed you to leave your country?

Poonam : I left India to come to France because I wanted to divorce. It was difficult. Nobody could help me. My family did not wish it either. I tried to see a lawyer who charged me 300 rupees in 1990, to tell me that if I had the chance to leave the country with my children, it was preferable for me to leave rather than to face the problems linked to the divorce. Divorce is never an easy business in India. The situation was very complicated. At that time, nobody had divorced in my family. It was something that was not to be done. My family had not accepted my marriage, so my divorce gave them a reason to say that love matches were not meant to work better than the arranged marriages. Quite to the contrary even. I obtained my divorce when I was already in France.

Question : Would you set out again to live for good in India?

Poonam : My life is with my children and I will live close to them. For the moment I feel very well living in Paris, where I live alone and free. It is a very cosmopolitan city.

Question : Do you miss India?

Poonam : With no doubt: yes. I go back each year there because I miss India very much. But I get a feeling of India here in Paris where there is an Indian district. I organize visits there on foot for those who are interested in Indian cooking and culture. I go to get my Indian films there. I found Indian restaurants, because it is not easy to cut off from your own culture. I spent thirty-three years of my life in India—it is a lot. Today, things have changed a lot with the Internet, the planes, and cheap flights…With so much globalisation in the world we can live wherever we want. However when I left India it was very difficult for me. But, I always felt rebellious.

RAVI: street kid

1st of December 2004 Dashāshvamedh ghāt.

If you walk on the ghāts of Kāshī, or on the streets of the old city, you will not be able to avoid these young children who do not go to school and wander around. Ravi is one of them. He spends his time playing with his kite, looking for money in the river and/or running after a hypothetical job's commission. At ten years old, Ravi is already a small man, to whom life has stolen his childhood.

Question : What is your name?
Ravi : My name is Ravi.
Question : How old are you?
Ravi : I am ten years old.
Question : Where were you born?
Ravi : I am born in Kāshī. All my family is from here. But my parents, my brothers live in the other side of the Gangā. I have 2 brothers. I am the oldest one.
Question : What do your parents do?
Ravi : My father is a boatman, and my mother stays at home looking after my brothers. My mother is very nice.
Question : Do you have many friends?
Ravi : Yes of course, many, many friends from everywhere.

Question	: What do you do during the day?
Ravi	: Today, absolutely nothing. Sometimes I play kite. Yesterday I brought flowers. Sometimes I sell little statues of gods. I don't sell postcards. Now this business is finished for me. I never need money. Money comes one day and goes away the next day.
Question	: Several times I have seen you taking out money from the Gaṅgā river with some kind of magnet. How do you do that?
Ravi	: I take a "chumbak" which is a magnet, (often taken from radio sets), and I put it into the water to take out money. Then I can buy some food, and when money is gone, I go to sleep.
Question	: Where do you sleep?
Ravi	: Most of the time I sleep there. It is my best friends' place. (He shows me the place, but it is just a space located under two or three umbrellas leaning against a wall.) That is my room. Sometimes I sleep at home—one night per week.
Question	: Do you love and respect your parents?
Ravi	: I love my mother very much, but my father drinks to much alcohol. Sometimes he is drunk. I hate alcohol; it is a very bad thing. I don't like people who drink, but my father is a good father, he does not hit me.
Question	: Why don't you go to school?

Ravi	: I have some problems. Money problems. I have no money for school, my father has money, but he drinks all the time, so no money for school. If I should have money, I would like to go to school with a lot of pleasure. I'd like to go to school, but it is not possible now. Up until two years ago, I went to school, when I was younger.
Question	: Your friends, are they going to school?
Ravi	: I have many friends and they don't go to school. My friend, Pravin, went to school but now he has quit, because he prefers to earn money. Hotels or silk shops give 25% commission. When he has 1000 rupees of commission, he does not go to school anymore. It is great to earn money. When I see a tourist, I also think about my commission. Usually families give money to feed their children, but not for education. When the parents see the money earned by their children, they think that it is better to earn money, so children don't go to school, because every family need money.
Question	: What do you want to become later on in your life?
Ravi	: Nothing. Maybe, having a silk shop, doing business.
Question	: Do you think about the future?
Ravi	: When I have enough money, then I will go to school.

204

Question	:	What do you think about Kāshī?
Ravi	:	It is a very nice place.
Question	:	Do you take a holy dip everyday?
Ravi	:	I immerse myself everyday into Gangā. Ten minutes. I don't do my prayers. But I go sometimes to one temple only, the monkey temple because I like Hanumān (the monkey-god), and it is a very beautiful temple.
Question	:	What will happen for you in the future?
Ravi	:	I don't know. Maybe I will look for God.

CYCLE-RICKSHAW DRIVER

The means of transport most frequently used by Banārsīs is the rickshaw. However, even if this means of transport is quite practical for travelling, these men who pedal all day long in pot holed and dusty streets have a particularly harassing job. To know better about them, we met one.

4th December 2004

Question	:	What is your name?
Rickshaw-driver	:	Shyam.
Question	:	How old are you?
Rickshaw-driver	:	I am twenty-five years old.
Question	:	How long have you been a rickshaw driver?
Rickshaw-driver	:	I started this job at the age of ten years.
Question	:	Where were you born?
Rickshaw-driver	:	In Bihār, Patna.
Question	:	Are you the owner of your rickshaw?
Rickshaw-driver	:	No, I rent my rickshaw. I have to pay everyday for that. Rent is twenty rupees for twelve hours.
Question	:	What is the fare for one kilometre?
Rickshaw-driver	:	In general ten rupees maximum, for Indian customers it's five rupees only.
Question	:	Is it the same price if there are one, two, three or more people on the rickshaw?
Rickshaw-driver	:	The price is five rupees per person per kilometre. It's more expensive because it's harder for me.
Question	:	In general what is your salary at the end of the day?
Rickshaw-driver	:	150 rupees, 200, 300, it depends on the day, if I am lucky or not.
Question	:	How many rupees is it for a good day?
Rickshaw-driver	:	150, 200. I get 300 on very, very lucky days or nothing on bad days.

Question	: Isn't it dangerous to be a rickshaw driver, because of the traffic?
Rickshaw-driver	: Yes, we have very big problems with the traffic. I am a small man- it is very difficult for me. So we have problems also with the police. Sometimes policemen beat us.
Question	: Why?
Rickshaw-driver	: Sometimes they beat us without any reason. We don't do anything wrong, but it is like that, we have no power, no political source.
Question	: What is the hardest aspect in your job?
Rickshaw-driver	: I have many problems with this job but I don't know how to get another job. I send all my money to my family who is in Delhi and Patna. I would like to have another job, but I know that it is impossible for me.
Question	: But what is the most difficult issue with this job? Handling the traffic, the people, dust…?
Rickshaw-driver	: I think it is the big concurrence of the new rickshaw pullers coming from Bengal or Bihār. We have many problems with them. The new-rickshaw pullers have more customers than my old machine. People prefer to go on the new ones. And also the rickshaw drivers who have been working here for a long time have more customers and fewer problems with the police or the different authorities. They can give some money to the police, five or ten rupees to cross some places and the job becomes easier. I have been here for ten years but I still have problems. And I have problems with the older rickshaw-drivers. Policemen and traffic are the main difficulties of this job. There is a lot of corruption. Everyday I have to pay policemen 10 or 20 rupees to cross Godauliā and to come to Dashāshvamedh. Sometimes I know the policeman and he lets me go through.
Question	: There is a lot of dust. Is it not unbearable? Temperatures can be very hot …
Rickshaw-driver	: For these reasons, it is very hard work. Sometimes I am ill because there is too much dust, to much pollution, too much heat.
Question	: Are there relationships good among the rickshaw-drivers?
Rickshaw-driver	: Ten rickshaw-drivers are from my family. But, here there are brawls often between rickshaw-drivers because of competition. The inhabitants of Kāshī have their

regular rickshaw-drivers, but concerning tourists customers who pay much better, there are fights, even if we know each other.

Question : Is there any competition with auto-rickshaws?

Rickshaw-driver : Not at all, people who want to take auto rickshaws, take auto rickshaws, people who want to take cycle-rickshaws, take cycle-rickshaws. It depends on the distances.

Question : Would you like your children to do the same work as you?

Rickshaw-driver : I have a fourteen-year-old boy and a three-year-old girl. I don't want my son to do the same work because it is really too hard. I come from a very poor family. My father did not care of us. And, I do not wish that it'd be the same for my children. I have to care for my family and provide for their needs. I would like my children to have a good work, more pleasant than mine and that brings back more money. I want to prepare them a nice future.

Question : You left your family in Patna. You came to work in Kāshī. Is it because of poverty?

Rickshaw-driver : Patna is a small city. Few tourists come to visit the city and it is necessary for us to go to bigger cities to earn more money. Bihar is a very poor province.

Question : Why do some rickshaws look so beautiful?

Rickshaw-driver : Some rickshaws are very beautiful and new. The dream of all rickshaw-drivers is to buy their own new rickshaw, one that works well and without problems. Because when you have your own new rickshaw, you have more customers and more money. We have a lot of mechanical problems with old rickshaws.

Question : Do you have health problems with this job?

Rickshaw-driver : I have a heart problem. And also, because I smoke Ganja. When I smoke Ganja, it's like medicine; I forget all my problems and also my fatigue. After that, I drive my rickshaw like a helicopter. It's like the gasoline for auto-rickshaw. But I know that it is not good for my health. But I don't drink any alcohol I only smoke Ganja…

Question : Since when and until what age can you be a rickshaw-driver?

Rickshaw-driver	: Many rickshaw-drivers begin at the age of fifteen. Work is not allowed for young people who are younger than fifteen, but many of them work. You have no problem with this job when you are young. But when you become older that becomes more difficult. I know a seventy year old cycle-rickshaw-driver. He is very old for such a job.
Question	: Do you need a licence or any authorization to do this job?
Rickshaw-driver	: Ten years ago, we did not need any licence, but now we need one.
Question	: Do you have to pay for this licence?
Rickshaw-driver	: Yes, the price is forty-two rupees per year.
Question	: Is the number of rickshaws limited?
Rickshaw-driver	: No, for that reason, there are many, many rickshaws in Kāshī. Too many rickshaws…I think that there are 100,000 cycle-rickshaws and 50,000 auto-rickshaws in the city.
Question	: What do you expect in your life now?
Rickshaw-driver	: I am waiting to have 5,000 rupees of savings to go back to Bihār. My dream is to go back there, and to see my family again. I am waiting for the help of the Gods to have a better life. But the Gods don't listen to me…

WRESTLER

Indian wrestling is a speciality of Kāshī. Traditional Indian wrestling has been around since the 6th century CE and is integrated within the religion of Hinduism. Indian wrestling also known as Pahalwani, Mallayuddha (Malla means wrestler and Yuddha means war or fighting) or Bharatiya

kushti is a form of exercise that defines the essence of wrestling and the wrestler, this term is mentioned in many Sutra. Through the eyes of Indian wrestling one achieves not only self discipline through physical fitness but also achieves identity and purity of the body, mind and spirit. Training takes place in the akhārā. When one enters the temple he leaves behind the civilisation he is part of and enters a world of tranquillity and acknowledgment. The akhārās are equipped with fine grit dirt floors to bring one closer to the natural elements of the earth. Dirty floors covering the training floor have been shifted and coated with essential oils to supple the skin of the wrestler when he is fighting. The oils also

208

keep the dirt clean and compressed for the bodies to tumble upon. Natural light and fresh air impact the training area as well to keep it in harmony with the surrounding atmosphere. Strength-orientated training is performed religiously. Indian wrestlers are well known for their flexibility and power. This is achieved through several types of exercises done with one's own body weight. Performing exercises such as Yogi (posture stretches), Bethak (in place squats), Dand

(push ups), Jori (sets of two cylindrical clubs, again, often huge, up to sixty kilos for swinging), Gada (swinging weighted ball and mace, Gadas are like huge lollipops, a bamboo stick attached to a ball of stone) as well as body massages give the wrestler a complete regime. The wrestlers are fed with a lot of ghī (clarified butter), considered to strengthen the body. Their body is massaged and coated with oil to soften the movements and make him more difficult to be caught. The wrestlers seldom wear more that a loincloth (a janghiya). Wrestlers pray to various Hindu gods, the two most important ones for the wrestler are Hanumān and Krishna

24th November 2004, 7am, Dashsvāmedh ghāt.

Question : What is your name?
Wrestler : My name is Shiva.
Question : How old are you?
Wrestler : I am thirty-one years old.
Question : Were you born in Kāshī?
Wrestler : Yes, I was born in Kāshī.
Question : You practice the wrestling. How do you call this activity in Hindi?
Wrestler : This is a very old tradition. We call that Pahalwani, Mallavidya or Bharatiya kushti. In our family we have practised wrestling for generations. From our childhood we have practised the exercises of wrestling. We are called the Yadavas and we practise wrestling in the akhārās. I was ten years old when I started to practise wrestling. But it is a very hard sport because it is difficult to reach a good level and to get the body fit. Some wrestlers are young, but it is necessary to be already strong. It is a strange feeling. Even young people appear already older because this practice is exhausting. We practise these exercises with a gada, a kind of heavy stone, swinging it in front of us, and behind us, for hours.
Question : Is it a tradition in India to practice wrestling?
Wrestler : Yes, this is a very old tradition in Kāshī maybe since the Mughals' invasion.

209

Question	: Your father and your grandfather were also wrestlers?
Wrestler	: Yes of course.
Question	: Is there a particular God who protects the fighter?
Wrestler	: It is Hanumān who protects us. He is a Monkey God. And this is a sport of Monkeys. People who do this sport are like monkeys. Hanumān is a god with a very mighty power- he helps us very much.
Question	: Is there any difference between the spirituality and the body for you?
Wrestler	: Yes because it is Indian exercise, it is very hard. If you practice the wrestling like the Westerners, you do push-ups it is only physical. As for us, we go further in our practice. It is also a spiritual practice.
Question	: Do you do prayers, incantations, mantras or meditation before fighting?
Wrestler	: No.
Question	: Do you know how many wrestlers are there in Kāshī?
Wrestler	: There are many, many wrestlers. It is impossible to work out the figure because Kāshī is a very old city, and this tradition is very old, so many people practice the wrestling.
Question	: Are there more wrestlers in Kāshī than in other places in India?
Wrestler	: Yes, it is a speciality of Kāshī. That is really a deep part of our traditions, our culture and our way of life.

Question	: Are there any competitions?
Wrestler	: Yes, they are organised during the summertime. There is wrestling everywhere in the akhārās. The government also organizes competitions.
Question	: Are there many places for training?
Wrestler	: Yes, there are clubs where we do the training, we call these places: akhārās.
Question	: Do you need a diploma or a qualification to teach wrestling?
Wrestler	: Yes, national diplomas.
Question	: Are the wrestlers considered heroes?
Wrestler	: I think so. They are seen as heroes and respected by the people and children dream of becoming wrestlers. It is in our culture. This activity is very specific from this town.
Question	: When are the competitions organized?
Wrestler	: Usually, they take place during the summertime, in August, during the festivals. The wrestling takes place outdoors and often under the rain, because it is the monsoon time. The bodies are slippery and more difficult to catch. It is also crowded. Many people come to see the wrestling; sometimes there are really many people. People practise wrestling often for a long time, and the tickets are expensive, from 100 to 400 or 500 rupees.
Question	: Where do the competitions take place?
Wrestler	: Sometimes in Delhi or Mumbai for the national competitions, but most of the time in very simple places like our akhārā.

Question	:	Usually, how many hours do you need to train per day or per week?
Wrestler	:	It depends. But two hours per day is long enough to get a good physical condition.
Question	:	What is the link between the fighters and the caste of the milkmen?
Wrestler	:	The caste of the milkmen-wrestlers is called Yadavas. Everybody can practise this sport but traditionally the people of this caste practice the wrestling. Because working with the milk is very hard. They need to be strong, to have big muscles, because they must carry very heavy tanks of milk all day, by bicycle or on foot. They have to be fit and flexible. They breed cows and buffaloes. They have to produce, to transport and to sell the milk. In the past the only people who practised wrestling were from the Yadavas' caste, but today many people come from other castes to practise this sport.
Question	:	How do you call the equipment used for training? The one that you swing in front of you and behind you?
Wrestler	:	It is called gada. Hanumān played gada. It is for that reason that we call it gada. It has a lot of power. In the Mahābhārata or Bhagvad-Gītā, the Gods did not fight with guns but with gadas.
Question	:	Can you explain how to use this gada?
Wrestler	:	We can use it by swinging it with one hand or with two hands. We use it slowly at the beginning of the training with one hand to warm the body. Then we accelerate the rhythm more and more. There are several manners of handling it. We swing it from one side to the other, in front of ourselves, then we repeat the same exercise behind our back. And we start again doing it continuously.
Question	:	Can it be dangerous?
Wrestler	:	Sometimes we get it on the legs but you have to train so that you get quicker, stronger and at the same time more flexible. It's a good exercise.
Question	:	What kind of other exercises are there?
Wrestler	:	There are a lot of exercises. It depends on the people. Mostly we use the gada but we do also many push-ups, we raise weights, barbells…

THE BOATMAN

The boatmen are as the fishermen, the workers of Gangā. To work on the holy river is an honour but this job is not permitted to everyone. You have to belong to the boatmen caste (Jāti). These men, proud of their work, often know very well their city and their history. Anup is one of them, and he very kindly tells us about

his work. But just by looking at his hands, you can understand the hardness of his task.

1st December 2004, on the Dashsvāmedh ghāt.

Question : What is your name?
Boatman : My name is Anup Kumar. My full name is Anup Sahani. My father, grand father, father in law and all the men of my family were boatmen or had a job with boats on the Gangā river. We belong to this caste. Having another job is possible, but in my family everybody has chosen this job. I started this job when I was very young.
Question : How old are you?
Boatman : I am thirty-two years old now
Question : Where were you born?
Boatman : I was born in Kāshī, like everybody else in my family. I have five brothers and I am the youngest one. All of them are boatmen. I have been married for two years and I have one little baby, a boy.
Question : Do you want him to become a boatman?
Boatman : Maybe, if he wants to do this job. It is not a problem for me; he can choose any kind of work.
Question : How long have you been doing this job?
Boatman : I started this job at the age of twelve years. Before that time, I was going to school, but I started helping my father more and more. And it became my own real job. I had my own customers, my own boat.
Question : Are you the real owner of your boat?
Boatman : Yes, of course. Actually, my father, my brothers and I, we have seven boats altogether. If I use my boat, I take all the money for me, but sometimes I have to rent a bigger boat and I have to pay one part to the owner.
Question : How much is it for a one-hour boat trip?
Boatman : Our prices are never fixed. It depends on the number of customers. Sometimes they pay fifty rupees, sometimes five hundred rupees. Sometimes groups need a guide and I also do that. I have a lot of knowledge concerning Kāshī. My father taught me this a long time ago. So I give a lot of information about Kāshī, the ghāts, and the history. I have to speak other languages: English for tourists, but also Bengali, Tamil, different Indian languages. So the price is more expensive. Sometimes the hotels take a commission (it can be 45%). Sometimes people just want to see the landscape and take pictures with their camera. Sometimes they just want to go swimming. So it is never the same price...
Question : Do you think that there are too many boatmen on the Gangā river?

212

Boatman	:	Yes, certainly. There is too much competition between the boatmen. All along the ghāts there are many boatmen who accost the tourists.
Question	:	Are the prices the same during the Monsoon and can you do a boat trip then?
Boatman	:	During monsoon time we need to have three people on the boat because the currents are very strong. For the big boats, we need four people to mano-euvre it.
Question	:	Can it be dangerous during the monsoon time?
Boatman	:	Not at all! It is like a train trip. Sometimes they go off the rails. It's up to your Karma…That is the same for boating. If god wants you to die today, you'll die…If it is not your day, you'll have to wait for another day. I am Hindu, I believe in that.
Question	:	What can you see floating on the River Gangā?
Boatman	:	You can find everything. This is the old city of Shiva. When a cow dies, people take the cow by rickshaw and then they immerse it with a stone into the River Gangā because they are considered as Gods. But sometimes they come up to the surface. There are also the dead bodies that are not burnt. It can be people who have not had the sacred fire in the burning ghāt, because they have no money to pay.

It can be a sādhu- that means a holy man. They are already pure, so they don't need cremation. They are dropped in the middle of the Gangā in the lotus posture, which is the meditation position. Also the newborn babies are immersed into the Gangā without cremation, because they cannot have bad Karma. Lepers don't need cremation either. We can also see dolphins jumping on the water. They clean the River Gangā.

Question	:	Are there still crocodiles, as we can read in some legends?
Boatman	:	A long time ago there were a lot of crocodiles. Now there are not many crocodiles. You can see some of them during the monsoon time, near the Asi ghāt or near the Varuna. They don't come to the city.
Question	:	Are there a lot of fishermen on the river Ganges?
Boatman	:	Yes, because there are a lot of fish, small fish, big fish. I also go fishing. Sometimes you can take a fish with your hand. Most of the time you fish with nets. Now with pollution there are less fish than five or six years ago. It is worse and worse. There are some campaigns fighting against pollution, but it is really difficult. Near the ghāts, on the banks, some people collect polluting material like plastic, flowers and so on, they keep it on the boat, and then

they go to the middle side of the Gaṅgā river to drown it back into the water. I cannot approve this way of cleaning the Ganges.

Question	:	Do you earn a lot of money with this job?
Boatman	:	Sometimes it's good, sometimes not good. It depends on the days. If God gives me one rupee, I am happy. He gives me 500,000 rupees, I am happy. I don't cry if I earn nothing on a working day. It is like that.
Question	:	Do you think it is hard work?
Boatman	:	It is true. It is a very hard work. Look at my hands.
Question	:	Are there some accidents on the River Gaṅgā?
Boatman	:	It is rare. But sometimes there are too many people sitting on the boat. They put fifteen people in a boat where only eight people can fit in. They are not prudent. And the River Police don't do anything.
Question	:	Do you need a boat driving licence?
Boatman	:	You can work in this job only if you are from the boatmen's caste. That is our licence.

SANSKRIT STUDENTS

For millenniums, the city of Kāshī holds a very high reputation as far as knowledge is concerned. It is the city of knowledge. And knowledge in India was transmitted for a long time through that particularly complex language, called the Sanskrit. The Vārānaseya Sanskrit Vishvavidyālaya is the flagship of Sanskrit teaching. But tens of other colleges or other schools teach it too. These days, to study this ancient language with so much enthusiasm and determination seems to be an incredible challenge. However, there are thousands in Kāshī and millions all over India who study it. This is why we went to meet two young students who think that Sanskrit is far from being a dead language.

Wednesday 15th December 2004: Dashāsvamedh ghāt.

Question	:	What is your name?
Sanskrit students	:	My name is Kamal . My name is Gyanendra.
Question	:	How old are you?
Sanskrit students	:	I am 19 years old. I am 16 years old
Question	:	Where do you come from?
Sanskrit students	:	I come from Manipur, in the north-east side of India. Next to Darjeeling. I am from Nepal, from the district of Jhapa.

Question	:	It is surprising for a Westerner, who lives in a modern world of sciences and computers, to meet somebody like you who is interested in a very old language, a dead language such as the Sanskrit's language. What is your interest in it?
Sanskrit students	:	It is not surprising because it is needed by all Hindu people, because the priests need to understand the Sanskrit's language. But everybody wants to study Sanskrit. Kāshī is a very holy place, the holiest place for Hindu people.
Question	:	Is it possible for you to be a priest without learning the Sanskrit's language?
Sanskrit students	:	It is impossible and we have to learn it very hard to succeed. This language is very difficult and we have to read many, many texts.
Question	:	For how long have you been learning Sanskrit?
Sanskrit students	:	I began six years ago. When I was thirteen years old. At the beginning it was very difficult but now it is much easier and more interesting. In three years time, I will have completed my Sanskrit subject, my Master of Art: M.A. But before that I want to be in a priest service or whatever God gives me. I am a beginner; I've just started one year ago. And it is now the most difficult time for me.
Question	:	Why do you want to be priests?
Sanskrit students	:	I don't want to be a priest, because I want to have a very high level in Sanskrit and in Hindi also. I want to become a lecturer at the University and teach Sanskrit. Same thing, I want to have my M.A in the Sanskrit subject and teach this language or another subject to other people.
Question	:	Is it only because you are a priest and a Hindu that you are interested in the Sanskrit's language?
Sanskrit students	:	The first reason is because I am a Brahmin. I am from the highest caste, the priest's caste, and I have to learn it. Kshatriya is another high caste, the warrior caste but they don't have to study Sanskrit. They go to the army. For my caste, the Brahmin's, it is a duty to become a priest and to learn very hard the holy texts. I have to read and understand also all the Vedas, all the mantras. My father wanted me to study well, it was very important for him.

Question	:	Are all your brothers doing the same?
Sanskrit students	:	Yes, of course. My brother is also in Kāshī, now he is in the temple, he is learning Sanskrit too, like everybody in my family.
Question	:	Did your family thought of another place for you to learn Sanskrit or was it the obvious place?
Sanskrit students	:	Absolutely not, this is the great place to learn this subject. You cannot think of another place. This is the most important place all over the world for Sanskrit studies. Sanskrit's teachers are excellent. The better professors are in Kāshī. They are very respected. It is an old and holy place. Everybody prays here, people from everywhere want to come here, they pray in the Vishvanāth temple, the golden temple.
Question	:	Do you also go to pray in the Vishvanāth temple?
Sanskrit students	:	Yes of course, we go to the temple. And we go to take the holy dip. Our Mother is flowing there. I am speaking about Mother Gangā of course. If the gods love you, they bless you and so they bring you there. There is no hazard.
Question	:	What are the most important texts written in Sanskrit?
Sanskrit students	:	The Bhagavad Gītā is an episode included in the sixth book of Mahābhārata. The masterpiece of the Hindu thought is about the moral advice given by Lord Krishna to Arjuna who is in despair because he has to take part in a battle where many of his friends and relatives have to lose their lives. It is a crucial text to know the life of traditional India and it is also a tale about Hindu ideals. There is also the Bhagavad Mahapuran and the Vedas. These are the texts that I am studying. Everybody wants to be like Arjuna, the best warrior, a great hero with bow and arrows. Lord Krishna gave us a lot of education about what is inside the world, about what the people were doing before, what happened before. And it helps us for the future.
Question	:	Is it very important for you to know these books, to know your history, to know things about your culture, your religion?
Sanskrit students	:	It is very important. Sanskrit and religion are very close. What Lord Krishna said was a very, very strong lesson and for many years. If we know the Gītā, if we know

216

our past, we will know about what will happen in the future. Knowing the past is a necessity to go towards the future. With the Sanskrit language, we can understand better our Indian culture.

Question : Are they non-religious texts written in Sanskrit?

Sanskrit students : Everything can be written in this language. You can find texts about philosophy, texts about medicine, also novels.

Question : Do you think that Sanskrit is a dead language?

Sanskrit students : Before, everybody wanted to learn Sanskrit to read and to talk in Sanskrit, like now for the English language. It is for that reason that there are many, many schools and Universities of Sanskrit in India.

Question : Do you speak with other people in Sanskrit?

Sanskrit students : Yes of course. In the Sanskrit University, we talk in Sanskrit, like in Hindi or in English like with any language, which is alive. But it is hard; you have to get a high level of study. Now the studying of the Sanskrit language is increasing. Many people have an interest in this language. Everybody wants to learn it.

Question : What are the subjects that are studied in Sanskrit?

Sanskrit students : Mantras, grammar, philosophy, mathematics, astrology (jyotish)… The Sanskrit grammar is particularly difficult to learn, very complex. The grammatical structure of Sanskrit is difficult for beginners. We are studying almost all day long. From very early in the morning. Then we do prayers and readings, but it is also in Sanskrit.

Question : From which part of India or from which part of the world are students coming from?

Sanskrit students : They are coming from everywhere in India but also from Nepal, from Bhutan, Sikkim and there are also many western students. But there are also other places to learn Sanskrit like Haridvār, Dvārkā …

Question : Can you tell us the names of great authors who have written in Sanskrit?

Sanskrit students : Vyāsa, (who has written the Bhagavad Mahapuran, the Mahābhārata), and Kālidāsa (375-415) (Sanskrit poet and philosopher). Both of them are very important authors.

Question : How many years of studies do you need to have a good level in Sanskrit?

Sanskrit students :	Around ten years. We have to work very hard during this time because we want to succeed. But you can learn during all of your lifetime if you want to.
Question :	After these ten years what do you want to do?
Sanskrit students :	We want to go back to our cities to teach Sanskrit and to perpetuate the use of this language, and of this culture. This way, Indian culture and also this beautiful language will never die.

KRISHNA KANT SHUKLA

Poet, scientist and musician, Krishna Kant Shukla is a peculiar man. His thinking is at the crossing of faith and science. His trajectory is atypical. During his youth he went to the schools of Kāshī before perfecting his studies in England and then in The United States. As a physician, he taught sciences there in a large American University. At this point in time he was living in a privileged environment and got gradually closer to his own culture and rediscovered there more particularly the texts by Kabīr. Fascinated by the poet, he immersed himself

in the texts of the thinker, and appreciated their value and their relevance. In the light of his scientific education, he confronted faith and science by never putting them in opposition. Continuing his research, he left The United States and returned to Kāshī to settle down there. From now on he devotes his life to the singing of Kabīr's poems of which he has become a great specialist.

SOME KEYS TO UNDERSTANDING KĀSHĪ:

Krishna Kant Shukla: When you really go deep, deep trying to understand Banāras, things start to make sense. Nothing makes sense to somebody who is not deeply grounded in spirituality and whose life is not centred in the divine. Somebody could be catholic, could be of whatever religion or not religious, what counts is spirituality. Then Banāras starts to make sense. You need the key to discover the secrets of Banāras. And if you don't have that key, it does not make sense, you just see the dirt, the corruption and the beggars, and the people who say: "where are you coming from?", try to touch you...

Shiva is a God. Shiva lives here. One of the names of Shiva is Bholā: "The innocent one". This is the beauty of Indian culture that we actually worship, qualities like compassion, like innocence. This god is like a child. The freedom of Banāras is like the freedom of the child. Children don't like to wear many clothes. The Banārsīs don't like to wear too many clothes. They want just to have a dhoti. Material things are not important. Even the merchants of the shops, they open the shops very late. They get up whenever they want, they go on the ghāts to meet friends, and they brush their teeth for half an hour. Even when they brush their teeth, they continue to speak to their friends. Even if they have a shop which needs their presence early in the morning, they prefer to enjoy these moments. When you go anywhere in Banāras, you see all the fruit sellers on the same corner. If we think with a Western mind, if you want to sell fruit and there is a part of town where there is nobody selling fruit, I will think that if I will open my shop there, I will make more money. But then I will feel lonely. I will have nobody to talk with, nobody who thinks like me, or who does the same things as me. Loneliness is a problem in Western countries, especially in America. You have to pay $50 to a psychiatrist if you want to talk. I asked these fruit sellers why they install their shop at the same place, why they loose a lot of business. And even if there is competition, even if they try to attract the same customers, they help each other, they speak together, they can be connected together. It is that fun and that freedom that are more important than the material wealth. That is the reason why you can find thirty fruit sellers at the same place. This kind of solidarity is most important.

The Western thought is influenced by the theories of Darwin, the theory of evolution, "struggle for life", and the survival of the fittest. In America they say, "Dog eat dog". It is the law of the jungle. You see the multinational companies, the big corporations, the businesses, you see the politics, and this is the worldview. According to this worldview, life is cruel, nature is hard and raw, and you have to kill or to be killed. The food chain, that's the idea. But the ancient thought, which was shared by the native Americans, the Red Indians, by any culture which has survived thousands and thousands of years, like the Chinese culture, the Tibetan culture, the Indian culture, they don't have this point of view. Competition and exploitation are not the laws of life, competition and exploitation are there, but only as a variation on the basic theme of cooperation. The "clashing waves" of competion exist on a huge, deep, silent ocean of cooperation. Even the most objective scientists, when they say something, we should always remember that they are speaking with their own consciousness. That is the case for the Darwin's theories. I am a physicist; I have spent thirty-three years of my life studying and teaching physics. So I am saying that from my deep experience. The point of view of ancient Indians is about sharing, cooperation, and family connection. Now biological discoveries are supporting this. For example now, they found that if there is a lake, a tree, and another tree growing far away from the lake, the first one has a lot of access to water, but not too many minerals, because the minerals have been washed and absorbed by the lake. The other one is thirstier, it does not have enough water, but it has lot of minerals. Scientists found that the roots were exchanging together what the trees needed. Cooperation and exchange, sharing symbiosis that is one of the most important laws of nature. Darwin has not seen that, he just saw the relationships of domination between the beings.

Indian mythology, religion or spirituality comes from this point of view: sharing, and cooperation. Western points of view and Indian points of view are really different. Even Darwin came later on. Before that, it was the bible. Like all religious scriptures, the bible has been twisted, mistranslated, misinterpreted; it is what I call Churchianity, and not Christianity. The original source of Christianity, the bible has a passage called "the Genesis". The teaching of Jesus Christ is very different than what they teach now. In the Genesis book, God made the earth, he told Adam, "I give you all this planet, all these trees, all these herbs, all this water, all these fishes, I give you dominion over all my creation. You are the boss". When I read this passage, with my Indian background, I realized that the original words of God had been twisted. The passage has been written by humans who lusted for power and domination. I see the beginning of the world like a beautiful garden, and we are the gardener. The plants and the animals are our brothers and sisters. God gave us intelligence so we have to take care of them. This point of view is shared by all Indians but especially here in Vārānasī.

Question: Do you mean that the intuition in Indian spirituality is joining the scientist theories?

Krishna Kant Shukla: Yes and no. Because sometimes it seems like it is similar, the Indian spirituality says something like that but actually it is only coincidental, the very roots and foundations of sciences are materialistic. They raised the matter at the level of God. But we don't know what matter is. I can tell you that because I am a physicist. Actually the scientists are like priests. Science is like a religion, because it is a matter of faith. I can look at the sun. And I can say it is a ball of hydrogen and helium, it's just a dead ball of gas with thermonuclear fusion going on inside. In India, a sādhu can tell you "no, no, it is the light of god, the illumination of Brahmā, it has a personality, a consciousness, an intelligence. It will protect you, it will guide you". The scientists choose to believe that the sādhu is wrong. But scientists believe also in some theory like a faith, like a religion. They decided to believe that the sun is a ball of gas. The sādhu has chosen to believe that the sun is something alive. If you ask a physicist, a chemist, a biologist they will never give you the answer because they have only half knowledge. So they become really like fundamentalists. They will never accept what I am saying. The physicist can tell you: "sun is a ball of hydrogen". You can retort: "what is hydrogen? ", "Oh very good question, hydrogen is protons with electrons revolving around it." You can tell: "what is a proton? ", "It is some nucleons, etc…" And you arrive to the most little particle: the quarks but we can continue this conversation, and every time there is another particle. But we don't know the total beginning. If you ask a good physicist: "what is matter? ", he will answer you: "It is a mystery". Giving a name to something is not knowing this thing. If I have a neighbour, I just know his name, I never talk to him, I don't know his feelings, maybe tomorrow he might pick up a gun and commit suicide. And you ask me: "who is that man? " I can tell you: "He is John." I give you the impression that I know him very well. But I don't know him at all. Most scientists are like this. We give something a name, and then we think we know everything. But we don't. To be very honest, everything is not perfect. There is a lot of worship here in Banāras, but not enough spirituality. Too many empty rituals. Being religious to show off to other people.

Question: Is it what the poet Kabīr said?

Krishna Kant Shukla: Yes, it is why I love Kabīr. He was against hypocrisies. Many people go to the temple, but if there is a starving dog there, they will push it away. Or if there is a beggar who is asking for food, they say: "don't touch me, don't touch me". God has made beautiful roses, but he has also made poisonous plants. We have to accept that. It is not correct to romanticise Banāras, to romanticise India.

KABĪR:

Krishna Kant Shukla: Kabīr was born 604 years ago in Banāras. Nobody knows exactly the truth about him. In India people always exaggerate. But the legend says he was born from Hindus parents, for some reason, maybe they were poor, or maybe he was born under a bad astrologic sign. Children born on a bad astrological sign bring bad luck for all the family. They put him in a basket, and they put him in a lake called Lahar Tara. He was found by a poor muslim couple—Financially poor but not spiritually poor. The name of this couple was Nīmā (the woman) and Nīru (the man). They had no children. So they found this boy, and kept the child for themselves. It was a common practice at that time. The legend says that when he was a young man, he felt the need to have a guru. But he was raised as a Muslim. And the most powerful and famous guru in Banāras at that time was a Brahmin called Rāmānanda. The caste system was in place, so even if this guru were enlightened he would not give initiation to Kabīr. The main reason was that Muslims eat beef. Kabīr wanted initiation from this guru. Some people say that Kabīr went to the guru asking for initiation, and the guru said: "No. Go away, you are Muslim.". This guru used to give the mantra. Everybody knew that. This mantra is "Rām". But it is important to receive it after it has been charged by the consciousness of a divine, of an enlightened master. Kabīr wanted this guru to give him this powerful mantra. Kabīr thought: "What can I do?". Then he studied the movements of the guru Rāmānanda like a spy. And when it was very early in the morning, four o'clock is still dark, everybody was asleep. Rāmānanda was up and he went to the River, to Gangā. Kabīr put himself on the path of the guru. Early in the morning, it was dark and nobody could see anything. He lay down on the steps, on the exact path that the guru used to take. So the guru stubbed his foot on the prostrate Kabīr. And as a reaction, Rāmānanda cried: "Rām, Rām, Rām". It is a common thing. Even when Mahātma Gāndhi was shot, he took the name of "Rām". And Kabīr said: "Thank you Guru, now, I am initiated." Because traditionally, during initiation, you touch somebody, the guru touches or puts his hand or his feet on the disciple and he gives the mantra. Because this mantra and this guru were very powerful, Kabīr became very powerful in yoga and meditation. His poetry can be divided in two parts. In a very small section, he talks, which to me is the most interesting, he talks about his inner experiences, he talks about meditation, spiritual practice, he gives a beautiful poetry which is incredibly powerful. Beautiful descriptions of what he sees in his meditations. I have translated in English many of those poems. When I give my concerts, before I sing, I give the translation. The other part is the social aspect of Kabīr; this part was very controversial during Kabīr's life. He was fearless. He became so famous and so powerful in his own lifetime, and so great.

For the Indian thought, time is like a river, it can become slow sometimes, it can become very fast, not like in Western countries where people think that time is linear, time is like a clock. We have thousands and thousands of scriptures, but the authors never wrote their names, they gave the names of some gods, but not theirs. To be humble is very, very important. The opposite of the cult of the ego. In America, you have to sell yourself. In India, even today, you have to be humble. The cult of ego is not accepted. So people who write beautiful pieces, nice poetry, or make a nice painting, they would not indicated names. 99% of Indian literature is like that. So it is very hard to create a sense of history. And all the history that they teach in Indian Universities and colleges is the history of India written by western scholars, British, German or French.

Kabīr in some social poems he equally criticizes Hindus and Muslims. He has never denounced Hinduism or Islam. Actually, Kabīr is very respectful, but he criticised the distortions of religions, the hypocrisy, the abuses and the exploitation of both religions. For example, Kabīr said: "Why the muslim priest is shouting like a rooster? Does he think that God is deaf?". He was also deeply against the cast system. He told the people: "Wake up!" If you read Kabīr's poems, it's like taking a cold shower of the spirit. It's really refreshing. People want to die in Banāras. Because if they die in Banāras, they will go to heaven, so in one poem is said, I will not die in Banāras. There is a place called Magahar. The legend says that if you die there, you are reborn as a donkey. Kabīr wanted to die there. "I have the name of God, I have the mantra. If I die in Banāras then who is going to say that the name of God is important? People will say you don't need to remember the name of God". So Kabīr died in Magahar.

Unfortunately the thought of Kabīr is not alive in Banāras today. It is like the people of Paris they don't go to the Eiffel tower. Many of them don't go to the Louvre. It is like in Greece. How many people remember Socrates, or Aristotle? A minority.

I can give you my own story. I studied in Banāras when I was a young boy. I did not really know many things about Kabīr, just a few lines from some of his poems. It's only when I went to America, that I read Kabīr in English. The Banāras' education system, the Indian system is a British education system. When I was studying at the school in Banāras, I knew about the poems of Emily Brontė, Robert Frost…But I did not know about Kabīr, about Tulsī Dās. And there are beautiful poets in the south: Tukaram the Kabīr of Mahārāshtra, and lot of other ones…Our poetry is absolutely fantastic. They are like Kabīr's twin brothers. When you meet people in Banāras, they tell you, "Kabīr, Kabīr, Kabīr", but they do not know Kabīr in fact.

KNOWLEDGE IN BANĀRAS.

Krishna Kant Shukla: Traditionally, Banāras was a place of knowledge for thousands of years, people wanted to study here. Like people in America who wanted to go to Harvard University, here in India, people wanted to study in Banāras University. But slowly, what happened in India is that the English rule was very long, 240 years, many generations. And before the British it was the Mughals. The strength of Hinduism is flexibility, acceptance and humility. The Christians have the Bible, Muslims have the Quran and Jews have the Talmud. They have just one book. Hindus have thousands of books. And when you read these books, there are opposite things. So it is very difficult for Hindus to unite, and to think like one. Unity is missing in Hinduism. And now the education system is basically the western model. My own experience, most of the people, even in Banāras are ignorant about our roots, about our language, our culture, the meaning about Gangā. "Mother Gangā, Mother Gangā", and then they throw plastic into the water. "Mother cow, Mother cow", and when cows eat plastic, they don't care about that.

There is a big University of Sanskrit, but they don't teach only Sanskrit there. I had to go to America to discover my roots and to find my love for Banāras and for India. It was the Americans who told me, "You have some things very beautiful in your culture. Look at your music, look at your religion…It is beautiful." Even if the people go to the temples, even if they practice, deep in their heart they are lusting for the west. The Westerners IN power told us that India is backward, a third-world country. They said that Hinduism was devil worship, that we are a poor country and that we have a disease country. We have corruption. We have pollution. It was the past. Now, we have computers, modern army, and nuclear bomb. The same Hindus who go to the temples, who worship the river, the Shiva lingam, were dancing in the street when the nuclear bomb exploded. They didn't realise that when a nuclear bomb explodes it also kills millions of animals. What about all these creatures, about these plants? Hinduism teaches us to respect life. It is like Georges Bush, he goes to church, he says he is Christian, but he goes and kills thousands of people in Iraq. And does he know that it is not the tenth commandment but the first commandment, which is not to kill? That is the same for Banāras, it is a very religious place, but the beauty is there. The spirituality is there, but is not easily visible. You have to pray hard to meet the real people of Banāras.

GANGĀ:

Krishna Kant Shukla: I know a place where the water is very clean. There is no bacteria. Water has been tested. I have seen the laboratory report. You have to go up stream 9 km. A very beautiful place. Shultankeshwar, that is the name. Gangā is the Mother. Mother gives you life and feeds you, takes care of you when you are sick. Our Gangā is like that. She gives so much life. She has a personality, she has consciousness and she responds. All the nature is like that. She is like a human being. The birds, the animals, the rivers, the mountains, the plants, even the rocks are like that. Because according to the

223

Indian philosophy, the supreme principle of creation is not dead matter but consciousness. Consciousness becomes the mind and from the mind comes energy and matter. So, the trees and the rocks and the rivers have consciousness and they have personality. I want to tell you a story of my experience. In America, I was walking in a forest, and I found a snake. I sat ten meters away from the snake, with my breath and my mind quiet, and with my mind I told the snake: "You are beautiful". Because everything in creation wants to be loved, to be appreciated, even the Gods, the mountains and the rivers also. Every creation. Everybody wants to hear: "Oh, you are beautiful, you are nice, I'd like to be with you. I love you.". It is absolutely what everybody wants. Because I am a scientist, I test everything. I told the snake: "You are beautiful, I enjoy the shine of your skin, the way you move is so great, and I would like to have you as a friend, I would be honoured if you would be my friend". Then the snake turned around, and went back into the forest. Then next week-end, I came back there, I said: "My friend the snake, where are you? This is your friend Krishna. I am coming, please come. After five minutes, he came. And I was so exited that I thought that nobody will believe me. I went back to see my friends. I said: "Next week-end", I told one of my friends, "you have to come with me, because nobody would believe me." She said: "Maybe the snake just lives there and goes in and out, we should go to another place to call the snake. Maybe the test should be more scientific." So, we went half a kilometre away from there, on the other side of the forest. And I sat down; I started to call the snake. fifteen minutes after, it did not come. And just when we wanted to leave, it came. Now, after this experience I know that it is true. Now, I don't need to read any books, I go and sit by the river, like I went to Gaumuk (source of Gaṅgā). And I talk to the river, I talk to Gaṅgā, she is my Mother. And she responds. She does not respond with sound, but I know she is listening. And when she wants to tell me something, she speaks through my own inner voice. When I went to Gaumuk, I did not wanted to pray for myself because my practice in life is to experience the meaning of unconditional love. I want to become the unconditional love. I don't want to just love somebody but be love itself. And I am very far from it. It is a very high aim, but this is my aim. I don't ask anything except love and devotion. I never ask in my prayers anything more than that. But I ask for others. I have friends. Somebody who is sick, somebody who gets divorced, very deep and old friends from college. I ask for other people. I went to Gaumuk, and I made fifteen prayers. Every prayer became true miraculously. If you are a modern Indian, a scientific minded modern Indian, then you would say: " This Mother Gaṅgā business, it is bullshit." Think of nature as a dead matter, or just chemicals interactions, it is not my way. For the scientist who believes that nature is just a construct of dead matter, nature will behave that way. It will be a self-fulfilling prophecy. But if you interact with nature as if she had a personality (a most beautiful and loving personality), she behaves that way with you. The first step in allowing magic into your life is to believe in it. For me this river is like a friend, like the birds, the mountains etc…When I sing, there is always a bird singing with me. And when I gave a performance in the place where Kabīr lived, a bird, a cuckoo, was singing on a tree just behind me. National TV recorded that, and you can clearly hear the bird. This is just what Carlos Castaneda said. This is why Mother Gangā is a mother to me, a very beautiful mother. But some Indians say that the river is a mother but they do nothing to clean the Gangā.

I have the same feeling for all the rivers but there is a special feeling for river Gangā. Even the scientists, who are involved with the study of Gangā, will tell you that there is something special, even if they don't believe in God. They tell that there is something unique in this river. If you go to the Gangā pollution laboratory, on Tulsī ghāt, they tell you that Gangā water has a special capacity. Bacteria don't grow in it. The bad bacteria die. Some scientists think that that's why when Gangā is flowing through the mountains; it picks up some silver and gold, some minerals. But, then when they remove all the minerals of the water, it still kills the bacteria. They think that maybe there is some bacteria which kills the others bacteria. So they put the Gangā water in a big pressure cooker which kills all bacteria, it becomes like distilled water, but for the Gangā water, they still found that bad bacteria doesn't grow in it. They make the scientific conclusion, that Gangā has something very special. They cannot say that Gangā water is holy, because they will loose their job, but there is something very special in this water. With my brother who has a PhD from Berkeley University, we did an experiment. We took one bottle of Gangā water, and other bottles of water from other rivers, lakes around Banāras, etc....He put bread with fungus into the different bottles. All the waters became cloudy. Fungus died in the Gangā water, it could not survive in the Gangā water. But the older people say that Gangā water is much more dirty than before. When I was a child, it was cleaner than today. I was going to swim in Asi ghāt, Tulsī ghāt. Now, I don't go to swim there.

ACTION BENARES

This city, whose beauty can take your breath away, shows poverty too. We were told about a group of health workers in white blouses who, every morning, walk along the ghāts. We already heard about them, but had never had the chance to meet them. Today we have Veronique Jaccard, a doctor of the "Action Bénarès" organisation, Laetitia, a twenty-five year old volunteer, Esther fifty-six year old, with her unfailing energy, Anja,

a young Berliner nurse, Papu, an elegant Indian with an overflowing kindness, Govind and Shyam, who are Indian Health workers and the rickshaw driver. Papu, Govind and Shyam are the permanent workers of "Action Bénarès". They have been working with Doctor Bernard-Yves Sabot (who has been in India for thirty-two years) for a long time (or Doctor Sab, as he is friendly referred to by the Indians). He is there with his wife Anna Sabot Ibanez, the heart and engine of "Action Bénarès". After having worked for Mother Theresa, he set up his own project Action Bénarès twenty-four years ago in

Banāras, where he has been living permanently for many years.

This December morning, the winter sun struggles to break through the clouds. We follow the "Action Bénarès" team. We descend the steps from one ghāt, and everyone places the metal cases—the emergency boxes—on the bare ground. There are pliers, scissors, compresses, bandages, antiseptic creams, Betadine, antibiotic powder, medicines…On top of that, a lot of goodwill. Just after having installed everything, limping people join the group. Lined up on two levels, they wait for their turn. Many are lepers. A tottering man approaches. He is handsome and proud with his beard and his jollyy glance. Two enormous bandages hold his calves and tibiae together. When Doctor Jaccard, aided by Laetitia, give him a clean dressing, two wide and deep wounds appear. However, I am told that they are healing well. A few weeks ago, the wounds were much more

pronounced and, thanks to the regular treatment, the recovery has been clearly positive. New volunteers are here, observing and they will follow suit when their turn comes. The patients have come closer, there is a relaxed atmosphere, and there are even jokes and smiles for the patients. There is always an encouraging word for them, advises on hygiene measures to be taken to avoid an additional infection. In the background, the temples stand up proudly in the blue-turning sky. Everyone knows that it will be necessary to return the day after tomorrow, to change the dressings and give reassuring words.

The working day has not ended yet. It gone noon and time to go, like every day, to the state hospital of Kabīrchaura. All the teams of "Action Bénarès" gather each day at noon to treat people at the hospital. A team arrives, transporting a large trunk on the white and red ambulance-like-painted "Action Bénarès" rickshaw.

In this hospital, where draughts come from everywhere, incantations, sounds of small bells reach us from the temple next door. "Action Bénarès" give their treatment here everyday. Doctor Sabot has managed to establish himself with his team here. They work for free. It is necessary to face the lack of space and means and the patients are poor. Doctor Sab and his team treat the Lawaris, who have no family, and also a burnt women. These women are burnt from head to heels. Their whole bodies are basically immense open wounds through which the flesh appears. This is due to the fact that in Banāras and its neighbourhoods nearly three thousand women die of criminally inflicted burns every year. In the majority of the cases, these burns, which they pretend to be accidental (the benzene stove exploded, the sarī caught

fire in the cooker…), are the result of actions perpetrated by the husbands or by the in-law family, for obscure reasons which are all related to dowry practices, despite being illegal since 1961. Often, these women die alone, the husband and the in-law family do not show up. Their own family, a sister or an aunt sometimes rally round them. Each day, the "Action Bénarès" team clean and treat the wounds. Each day, they alleviate these wounds of fire. Each day, their glances, their gestures and their words comfort those who will die. 20% of these women manage nevertheless to be saved. It is the hope of healing and comforting that stimulates Stéphanie and Esther, a sort of urgency that appears in their glances, compassion linked with action.

There is also the corridor of the orthopaedic department. It is the corridor of the crippled, those who have fallen from the roof of trains or have gone under the rail tracks. Julien decides to take out some patients on their wheelchairs. He takes them to the barber's and buys them some samosas.

The following day, we follow the team to the lepers' village. They set themselves up under a covered playground. Wooden props are used to place the limbs to be treated. The interactions are pleasant and sometimes funny. A woman and her children come to be examined. They do not suffer of leprosy, as it has been eradicated thanks to the vaccines and the Raoul Follereau Foundation. The younger generations have not been affected. Therefore, there are not just lepers here. The team treat all kinds of wounds with kindness and professionalism. Then, we follow them to the station. The surroundings are crowded with small groups. We enter the hall is crammed. The team is divided into small groups of two or three people in order to check all the nooks and crannies better. No need to walk too long to find the patients. The blankets are lifted to check if everything is all right. Here and there, there is a stop, a small injury, a big infected wound or to give some words of comfort. Laetitia takes off her gloves, and during all

the cures, she will stroke the forehead and the face of a child, whispering him comforting words. One notices the determination in the glance of this young volunteer, a kind of fuel for her engine. She does everything she can, makes tremendous efforts, fights against indifference, revolts, looks after, talks, smiles…She grows up. She comes out of this with increased stature. She is like these young adults who have joined the adventure of the "Action Bénarès": courageous and full of will…And most importantly: humble.

On the other side of the station, there is a shantytown. It is there where Papu and Veronique (Dr. Jaccard) have set what they call with derision "the clinic", i.e. a rope bed placed on the side of a dusty road. People arrive quickly. Lots of patients, many of them are victims of the violence that comes with poverty. In this scenario of global rejection, they are the drop of hope that cures the wounds of soul and body.

We also follow them to the shantytown of Durgā Kund. Each day of the week, the team goes there, cures, talks and advises. But today, like every Saturday, it is the children's going-out day. Stéphanie, Leila, Shyam and Julien embark some thirty children out of the shantytown. This Saturday's plan is to go to the temple of Rāma (Tulsī Mānas Mandir). Tactfully, Shyam takes the children to the next floor where many scenes of the Hindu mythology are represented with puppets and automats. Still wide-eyed after watching so many enchantments, everyone heads to the temple gardens. A statue of an elephant and a crocodile are used as a swing by the children. Everyone present is taken to a small cheap restaurant. After having washed their hands, everyone will be entitled to their chickpeas and potatoes dish. It is not only a way to give them a proper meal, but also to get them to socialize. It is a chance to take them out from their daily environment, to show them something different than the mud of the shantytown. But it is also an opportunity to identify possible diseases, malformations, deficiencies or any other type of problems linked with poverty, it is a way to prevent.

"Action Bénarès" is an organisation, which aims—regardless of religious and moral prejudices—to give free health care to those who are completely excluded from it, to go with those who have been completely abandoned by society, family and the system. Their working conditions are extremely difficult. They have two permanent and paid doctors, three paid Indians, some volunteers, a bicycle, a rickshaw and lots of goodwill, generosity, abnegation and love. This is how it works: the financial support from donations is used exclusively for the purchase of medicines and medical equipment, as well as the wages. Working expenses are particularly limited. All the volunteers have to pay for their travel, their accommodation and their food. Throughout the year, the volunteers share this adventure by giving some of their time and making the most of their skills. It is generosity in a pure form, bold devotion without anything in return. This is why, in this town of contrasts with infinite charms, we met pain and death…But also hope. Because from now on, we know that, in the middle of this darkness, a flame still burns and it shall not be extinguished easily. To keep it burning, do not hesitate, please contact them: www.actionbenares.com

EVERY DAY LIFE

CALENDAR:

Apart from the Gregorian calendar, used in the public office and most of the economic sector, several calendars are used

The 12 Indian months of the year are:

Chaitra (March / April)

Vaishākha (April / May)

Jyeshtha (May / June)

Āshādha (June / July)

Shrāvana (July / August)

Bhādrapada (August / September)

Āshvina (September / October)

Kārttika (October / November)

Mārgashīrsha (November / December)

Pausha (December / January)

Māgha (January / February)

Phālguna (February / March)

The 12 months are divided into 6 seasons:

Vasanta (spring)

Grīshma (summer)

Varshā (rainy season)

Sharad (autumn)

Hemanta (winter)

Shishir (cold season)

The days of the week are similar to ours. The month is divided into two fortnights set by the moon: one is bright (shukla) and one is dark (Krishna).

FESTIVALS

Rakshā Bandhana

Celebrated in Shrāvana (July/August) This is celebrated in North India. On this day a sister ties a rākhī (silken amulet) on her brother's right wrist and wishes him good luck and protection from evil. In return the brother gives gifts to his sister, the value of which is not counted in material wealth but symbolic. The brother also vows to protect his sister.

This is also the day when old sacred threads (Janeū) worn by the three major Hindu castes (Brahmin, Kshatriya and Vaishyas are changed for new consecrated ones

Krishna Janmāsthamī

Celebrated in Shrāvana (July/August). This day is the birth anniversary of the eighth incarnation of Vishnu. According to the legend Vishnu incarnated himself as Krishna to destroy the evil Kansa who was harrassing mankind.

On Janmāsthamī, devotees keep a strict fast, which is only broken at midnight, at the time of Krishna's birth. Homes and Temples are cleaned and decorated and the life and exploits of Krishna are depicted in jhānakis (tableaux) in temples homes and in processions.

At midnight the idol of baby Krishna is placed in a decorted cradle and arati is performed. The image is ceremoniously bathed in a mixture of honey curds, milk, dry fruit and tulasī leaves (holy basil). The mixture is then distributed as prasāda and the fast is broken by partaking of it. On the preceeding day Hymns are sung in praise of Krishna, and passages from the Gītā and The Bhāgavat Purāna are recited.

Navarātra

Celebrated in Āshvina (September/October). This is a composite festival celebrated all over India. Beginning with the new moon in the month of Āshvina, this festival consists of fasts and worship of the nine aspects Durgā, one on each of the nine days. Durgā has 1008 names or epithets but is worshipped in her nine forms, which are sometimes interchangeable since basically they represent only her. The following are the most popular forms of the goddess. Durgā, Goddess of beyond reach; Bhadrakālī, the auspicious power of time; Amba or Jagadamba, Mother of the world; Annapūrnā, giver of food and plenty; Sarvamangala, aupicious goddess; Bhairava, terrible, fearful power of death; Chandrikā or Chandī, violent, wrath, fury; Lalitā, playfulness personified; Bhavānī, the giver of existence.

Navarātri the festival of nine nights is celebrated differently in different parts of India, during this festival she is worshipped as Shailputrī, Brahmachārini, Chandraghantā, Kushmānda, Skandamātā, Katyāyani, Kālarātrī, Mahāgauri, and Siddhadātri. She is also welcomed as Mahākālī for killing the demons, Madhu Kaitabha, who, for thousands years troubled Vishnu. She is also worshipped as Chāmundā for killing the demons Chunda and Munda.

Durgā Pūjā

Celebrated in Āshvina (September/October). First celebrated in Bengāl this festival has now spread to all parts of India especially where there are large Bengāli communities. During Navarātri celebrations this Pūjā really gets underway from the sixth day when the image of the Goddess is installed in highly decorated pandāls (tents or stalls). Some of these stalls are now fashioned into replicas of famous temples of the sub-continent. The preparations for this festival start months before with highly skilled artisans making the beautiful clay images of the goddesses. Being a holiday for most Bengālis new clothes and sumptuous dishes are the order of the day.

These pandāls are visted by thousands during the nights of the next three days until on the tenth day Vijayalakshmī the Image is taken with much celebration for the immersion ceremony in any one of India's rivers. Celebrated with great fervour in Bengāl it is the focal point of the year when annual holidays are celebrated in most concerns. Night long cultural programmes amongst other things mark this as one of the greatest cultural events in eastern India in particular.

Dashaharā

Celebrated in Āshvina (September/October). This marks the victory of Rāma over the demon Rāvana in Sri Lankā. During this festival a month long depiction of the story in the form of Rāma Līla takes place This Līla depicts all the major events of the Rāmāyana. This Līla is in fact performed throughout the whole of Southeast Asia. In India every town or city in North India has its own Līla. The most famous of these is the one held in Rāmnagar the residence of the Kāshī Naresh just on the opposite bank ot the River Ganges. This festival takes place during the Navarātra festival and culminates in the Vijayadashmi celebrations on the tenth day when Rāvana is finally defeated and killed by Lord Rāma.

Divālī

The festival of Divālī (or Dīpāvalī) takes place every year with the new moon of the month of kārttika (October-November). It is the festival of the lights. Divālī means line or row of candles (diyā: in Hindi).

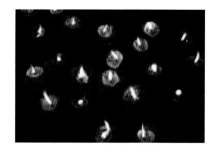 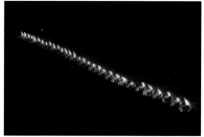

On the days preceding the festival, the Hindus tidy their houses and repaint the walls of their premises or their workplace. Divālī is the festival of light: during this night, people light candles of oil or ghī (clarified butter) in all the corners that remain dark. Divālī symbolizes the triumph of the light over the darkness, the triumph of knowledge over ignorance.

This festival originates in the legend of the Rāma god returning after fourteen years of exile in the town of Ayodhyā, having killed the Rāvana demon (who reigned on Lanka). People light candles in his honour.

In the Divālī event, people also celebrate Laksmī, goddess of prosperity and richness. So the shopkeepers and merchants repaint their stores to welcome the goddess who comes down to the Earth this time each year.

It is above all an occasion for a big celebration very dear to the Hindus. Indeed, small lights shine everywhere, but it is also a nightlong event of fireworks and crackers. The festival of Divālī symbolizes the victory of the light, and brings a message of peace and harmony to the world.

Dālā Chath

The festival of Dālā Chath takes place during the month of Kārttika (October-November), on the 6th day after the festival of Divālī. It is celebrated mainly in Bihār and by persons of Bihāri origin. That means that the Dālā Chath festival is celebrated during the sixth and the seventh days of the cycle of the crescent moon in the month of Kārttika. During this festival, women make offerings to the Sun god (Sūrya) and pray for the family, requesting prosperity and happiness.

Thus for two days, the women of the family gather on the banks of the Ganges to make their offerings (arghya). On the first day, this takes place at sunset and the second day, at sunrise. The offerings consist of flowers, fruit, vegetables and edible balls called "Pind", that are made of rice (chāval), flour and (khoā), a kind

milk boiled until it is hard as butter and sugar. These Pind offerings are made to honour the dead close relatives (father, mother, brother, sister, son, daughter). All the offerings are laid down in a basket generally known as Dālā and hence the name given to the festival.

Before placing these offerings, the women set up six sugarcane sticks joined together at the top (īkh), resembling a teepee. That forms a circle on the ground around which small lights (diyā), flowers, etc., are placed. The women take their place around the structure to pray and sing "bhajans", religious songs. This festival is very popular among the women from the province of Bihār. In Kāshī, millions of pilgrims meet on the banks of the Ganges, providing a very impressive scene.

Kārttika Pūrnimā

This festival takes place on the full moon (Pūrnimā) inthe month of Kārttika (October/November). Many small lights are lit in small baskets suspended from big bamboo poles in the Pancha-gangā ghāt. They illuminate the sky in memory of the deceased and light the way to allow them a safe return to the world of the ancestors. Millions of devotees attend to make their ablutions. Concerts are organized on the Rājendra Prasād ghāt esplanade. They also organize an āratī (offering of lights' ceremony) with many priests (pūjārīs).

Mahāshivarātri

The Mahāshivarātri festival is celebrated in the month of Phālguna (February/March), honouring the marriage of Shiva and Pārvatī.

The legend recounts that a poor fellow, a die-hard devotee of the Lord Shiva, who was looking for some firewood in a dark forest, could not find his way back home when night fell. In total darkness, he started hearing the cry of the tigers, and became very scared. He climbed onto the nearest tree, to be safe until the dawn. To avoid falling asleep, he gathered leaves from the tree, and dropped them to the ground while singing the name of Shiva, and some drops dripped from his flask, too. With the first sunrays, the man realized that the leaves and the water had fallen on a lingam at the bottom of the tree. Shiva liked that, chased away the tigers and blessed the poor guy. From that day, according to the Purānas, this tale is recited every night during the Mahāshivarātri festival.

The celebration of the Mahāshivarātri features a long-day fasting after keeping vigil the night before. They make the pūjā with milk and Mālābār orange-tree leaves whose fruit is the bael, known as bael patra. The women celebrate in a particularly enthusiastic manner. The married ones pray for their husbands and sons. The girls pray to have an ideal husband, someone like Shiva. They thus imitate Pārvatī who, according to the legend, prayed and practised the austerities (tapas) all day long to protect her husband Shiva from the dangers of the moonless night.

According to the holy texts', the offerings to the Lord Shiva must include bael leaves, which calm the hot-blooded divinity and represent the purification of the soul, vermilion paste (kumkum)—that represents the virtue and coats the lingam—food (that favours longevity and the fulfilment of the desires), incense (supposed to bring abundance), a lit lamp (favouring the acquiring of knowledge) and betel leaves, representing the satisfaction of the profane pleasures. The devotees go in crowds to the temple of Vishvanāth but also to other temples where they practise their pūjā, and pay a homage to the lingam itself by covering it with flowers, milk, honey, sandalwood paste and water from the Ganges. This festival is very impressive for the number of pilgrims it attracts, in millions, to the Holy City. For this occasion and in the honour of Shiva, a strong consumption of bhāng (preparation containing cannabis) is noticeable.

Holī

This very popular festival announces the arrival of the spring in the month of Chaitra (March/April). The legends, (there are many) surrounding Holī are narrated by the eldest, the day before the festival, around a large fire called Holikā. With full moon, this fire is lit in order to banish the evil spirits. These bonfires recall the putting to the stake of the witch Holikā. According to the legend, Holikā was immunized to the fire. She despised prince Prahlād for his devotion to Vishnu and plotted to destroy him by attracting him into an inferno. Unfortunately for her, the gods intervened and her magic was turned against her. Once the smoke had disappeared, Holikā was nothing but a pile of ashes. For Holī, the houses are cleaned, repainted and decorated. People buy new clothes. On the day of the festival, people come to the streets and throw water and coloured powder at each other. This festival symbolizes fecundity and carnal love. It is a day of cheerfulness for all the Indians, a chance to treat themselves with sweets and to let themselves go.

THE HOLY COW

According to the legend recounted in the Bhāgavatam, Kāma-dhenu, the celestial cow holds the gods within. Indeed, at the beginning of times, the Gods and the Demons decided to churn the Primordial Ocean of Milk in order to extract the Nectar of Immortality (Amrita) from it, which would ensure their supremacy. They chose, as a churn, the  Mount Meru, residency of the Gods, and placed it on the back of Kūrma, the Tortoise (the god Vishnu's second avatar). They asked the long snake Vāsuki to be the  rope of the churn. The Gods got together at one tip of the rope, the Demons on the other, and they began the churning. Wonders started to happen, then, in the Ocean of Milk, one of which was the famous nectar of immortality. Among the wonders, a miraculous cow came out of the Ocean. Its body encompased all the gods. It

was, according to the legend, the celestial Kāmadhenu cow, whose

generous udders provided milk in abundance to the whole humanity.

Seals dating from the age of the valley of Indus (2600 BC-1500 BC) were found. They depict animals in a suggesting their worship and holy attributes. There are drawings of cows predicting the future sacred character the Hindus allot to them.

The respect for the cow is one of the manifestations of the Hindus' attitude towards all living beings: human, animal, vegetable and even mineral, it is its symbol. Indeed, for the Hindus, the divine presence is immanent in all things and all creatures. This is why the town of Kāshī does not depart from the rule. And while walking along the tiny streets or lanes, one mixes permanently with the cows. It is not rare to see some of them running everywhere or nicely lying under the sun, having a nap. The inhabitants save the leftovers or vegetable leaves for them. They provide to some extent, the refuse collection. Lazilly, they trail in the area around the markets. Some bear red powder traces (kumkum) on their foreheads like a blessing. Others proudly bear garlands of flowers (mālā). Pilgrims, after having touched it, take their hands to their forehead while others put handfuls of rice on their back as an offering. One could think that they wander the streets without any owner, but this is not the case at all. Because all these cows belong to somebody, and most of the time, alone or accompanied by their owners, they return quietly to the cowshed when the night comes. In the countryside, the cow is used in the fields as a working tool, whereas downtown, the milk it produces is an essential supply for the family life. The Indians, who are vegetarians, are very fond of milk delicacies or other dairy products such as butter, ghī (clarified butter) or yoghurt and other fresh milk products. Its nutritional contribution is a significant element of food. Cow dung is collected and dried to be used as a fuel. The cow, beyond its holy character, has thus a social role. And, undoubtedly, this has favoured the rise of the animal to a divine rank. So it is easy to understand why eating the flesh of such a precious animal is regarded as a serious offence, a blasphemy. Besides cows, bulls are also numerous in Kāshī. Their corpulence is often very impressive. It should be added that the bull is also very fondly venerated, not only as the male form of the cow, but also as the vehicle of Shiva, or more commonly called Nandī.

INDIAN PRECURSORS

India is believed to be the oldest existing living civilisation. The town of Kāshī is one of the oldest cities that have always been inhabited until today. It is right to think that the Sanskrit, the language of Veda, is the mother of all European languages.

Aryabhatta (476), Varahamihira (505), Brahmagupta (598), Bhaskaracharya (600) are distinguished mathematicians who made great contributions to scientific progress. "We owe a lot to the Indians, who taught us how to count, without them, no scientific discovery could ever have been made", said Albert Einstein. The zero, this capital concept was invented by an Indian mathematician. Brahmagupta defines the zero as being the result of the subtraction of a number by itself. Bhaskaracharya (5th century) worked out the time it takes for the Earth to turn around the sun (365.258756464 days) hundreds of years ago, well before the Western astronomers did. Algebra, trigonometry and the calculus come from India. The quadratic equations were studied by Sridharacharya in the 11th century. The Greeks and the Romans could count up to 10^6 while the Indians counted up to 10^{53} (10 raised to the power of 53) with specific names, and this, as long ago as from the Vedic period (5,000 BC). The decimal system was developed in India in 100 AD. The value of the number pi was first calculated by Budhyana in the 6th century, a long time before the European mathematicians managed to do it. He explained the concept of what is known today as the Pythagoras Theorem.

The first university in the world was established in Takshashila in the year 700 BC. More than 10,500 students from all over the world studied more than 60 Subjects.

The University of Nalanda, built in the 4th century BC, was one of the greatest achievements of the ancient India as far as education is concerned. Buddha attended on several occasions. The Chinese scholar Hiuen Tsiang studied there.

When many other cultures were still nomads in the forests, 5,000 years ago, the Indians had established a system of agriculture in Harappā, in the valley of Sindhu (civilisation of the Indus valley).

Ayurvedic medicine is the oldest school of medicine. Sushruta is the father of surgery. 2,600 years ago, he and other scholars led serious studies on caesareans, cataracts, artificial limbs, fractures, urinary clots, plastic surgery and brain surgery. The use of anaesthesia was well known in ancient India. More than 125 items of surgical equipment were used. The knowledge of anatomy, physiology, aetiology, embryology, digestion, metabolism, genetics and immunity was also spread.

India was the richest country on Earth until the Muslim invasions in the 10th and 11th centuries and finally with the coming of the European traders especially the British in the 17th century who not only exploited but also colonised the sub-continent. Christopher Columbus became attracted by its richness.

Chess (Shataranja or Ashta Pada) was invented in India.

Even today, Indians enjoy a worldwide prestige:

The creator of the Pentium system is Vinod Dahm (90% of the computers work nowadays with a Pentium processor).

One of the two founders of Hotmail (the e-mail software, the world's no 1 Internet messenger system) is Sabeer Bhatia.

India is currently the greatest democracy in the world.

SMALL TRADES

What characterizes Kāshī, just like any other Indian city, is the utmost profusion of small trades. Thousands of tiny shops mark the lanes of the old city (Chauk). Some are just simple and tiny niche embedded in the walls. All sorts of goods are manufactured and sold there. It goes from the pān-walla, the pān (betel) vendor, the seller of religious items or offerings, the mechanic or the pastry baker. The silk stores are often more spacious, because this trade requires to unpacking the fabrics, and the choice of the sārī is a woman's business, so decisions should not be made lightly. Often, many of them come together, and the lengthy unpacking can last hours, as the tradesman will be able to unfold his whole stock with an unrivalled patience. There is also the bīdīs salesman, these very popular Indian cigarettes, a craft made in the shops. They are fine cigarettes made of chopped tobacco,

then dried and finally wrapped in a shrub leave bound by a cotton thread. All are handmade. The craftsmen gather according to their trade, or Jāti (caste). The

jewellers, and other bangles salesmen (bangles are very popular among Indian women), or the bindis salesmen, who decorate women's forehead, are all based in the same street.

Fresh yoghurts and other milk product merchants gather among themselves. The clothes' shopkeepers remain among their peers; fruit vendors, among fruit vendors; baggage traders, among baggage traders, and so on and so forth. There are stationers who sometimes sell calendars that include all information about the stars, essential for everyone to make

right decisions. The flowers vendors and other copperware retailers and manufacturers sell their goods around the temples. The spice stalls are found along the lanes, scenting the air with their intoxicating fragrances. The scents lead the way. Small craftsmen work the wood, hand-making sandals, children toys, items traditionally used in weddings…People buy rice, the basic food ingredient in shops, where large open bags are filled with different types of grains. Teashops offer all varieties of teas. India is the biggest producer of tea in the world. When lunchtime comes, everyone hurries towards small rudimentary stalls (dhabas), where all the culinary specialities are found. Indians are fond of delicacies: samosas, chapātī, pakorā, jalebī…

At any time, the Banārsīs stop at the chāi shop to have a tea with milk, sweetened and aromatised, normally served in small clay

cups, and it is considered appropriate to break them on the floor once the beverage has been swallowed. It is possible to meet single

tea peddlers. The container, close to embers, always remains piping hot. Another vendor sells sugar cane juice squeezed by a large power-driven ma-

chine that sits imposingly on a cart. It is a very refreshing drink. Further on, an old typewriter indicates that you are at a public writer's. Men walk carrying huge baskets with

peanuts on their heads. On bare ground, on a street corner, a shoemaker repairs footwear and even flip-flops. Here, no-one throws away anything,

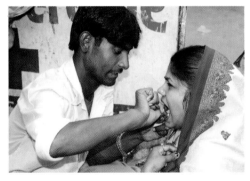

everything is repaired. The barbers and other hairdressers are innumerable in Kāshī, because

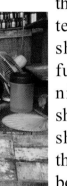

their services are often used for ritual shearing in all funerary ceremonies, or for the shrāddha, the worship dedicated to the dead as a symbol of purification. Sometimes, on the ghāts, it is also possible to come across ear cleaners, meticulous and very delicate. And it is not strange to be attracted by the tunes coming from the harmonium of a travelling musician. It is this life and this excitement produced by each trade that makes this city so attractive and captivating.

SILK AND SARĪS

India, and more particularly Kāshī are famous for its silk since the dawn of time. Already in the Rig Veda there are traces of silk production from around 1500 to 2 000 BC.

But mughals invasions stimulated the production. The sarīs of Kāshī are regarded as the most refined of the country, making it an almost compulsory wedding present. According to estimations, the sector (100% craftsmanship) employs nearly 125,000 people in the city of Banāras alone. Traditionally, silk was regarded as the purest fabric; this is why it was used

for rituals and to decorate the divinities in the temples. There are a large variety of sarīs: Jangla, Tanchoi, Vaskat, Cutwork, Tishu, and Butidar. The sarī is the traditional female clothing par excellence. Particularly smart, it is simply made of a long piece of fabric, five to six

meters long and 1.25 meter wide, approximately. It is

most commonly worn rolled up around the waist and covers the chest passing under the right shoulder, while the other piece is left loose on the left shoulder. The manufacturing materials (silk, cotton or synthetic), the colours, the patterns, the edgings, the "pallu" (top left end of decorated fabric expected to be seen), as well as the way of wrapping it around the body (depending on the areas) are extremely varied. It is in generally complemented by a long cotton underskirt (petticoat)

that ties around the waist, and by a tight blouse of matching colours. The silk sarīs of Kāshī are among the most famous. But silk production is far from being exclusive to the manufacturing of sarīs.

The brocades are pieces of silk enhanced with silver and gold thread woven designs. These threads are obtained by narrowly rolling up an extremely

fine silver or gold thread around a silk thread. These fabrics can be used for clothing or for furnishing. The drawn motifs are often of Mughal origin. They bear the names of "guldasta" (bouquet), "ambi" (mango or drawings known as Cashmere), "latifa" (flowers), "bel-buta" (ivy and buds), "badal me phul" (flowers in the clouds). Jamdani is a

famous silk muslin traditionally woven in Kāshī.

Whereas the sale of silk is mainly carried out by Hindu merchants, manufacture is mainly the business of Muslims.

While strolling along the lanes of Kāshī, it is not rare to pass by tiny workshops where trad-itional weaving looms are stored. Work is done exclusively by hand. But most of the production is carried out in the localities of Alaipura, Mandanpura and Lallapura. The salesmen are called "gaddidars" and the weavers, "karigars".

However, over the last few years, Chinese production has been trying to invade and take over the Indian market threatening an ancestral local know-how that has led hundreds even thousands of craftsmen to unemployment.

plate (tāvā). The chapātī is a common food in the north of India, where they are eaten with vegetable dishes, condiments, or simply with butter. The small ones are called phulkā. Fried in oil, golden and risen, they are the pūrī of the festival meals. Rotī is a generic term for the chapātī and their derivates, made of wheat flour or other components.

Nān: a speciality of Punjāb and Kashmir. This tasty and tender bread is made with flour, yeast, yoghurt and ghī, and then baked in a clay oven with wood (tandūr).

Parāthā: pancake prepared with whole-wheat flour, kneaded with water with a bit of ghī, and spread out with a roller several times to make into a kind

FOOD

Bread: Various kinds of unleavened and flat breads

Chapātī: a type of wheat flour pancake—whole-wheat or half refined (ātā)—salt and water, of a rather elastic texture and a rich taste, cooked on a curved cast iron

of puff pastry. It is cooked like the chapātī on the cast iron plate, or tavā. It can be eaten on its own (plain parāthā), or stuffed with potatoes (ālū parāthā), with cauliflower (gobhī parāthā), spinach (sāg parāthā), etc. Served with the morning tea, it constitutes a very tasty and substantial breakfast.

Snacks

Masala dosa: strongly spiced vegetables wrapped in a lentil and rice flour pancake.

Pakorā: chickpea flour fritter (besan) stuffed with onions, potatoes, aubergines, cauliflower or spinach, served as munchies with tea or as a starter.

Samosa: triangular turnovers stuffed with vegetable curry.

Sabji: Vegetable dishes (vegetable curry)

Alu chhole: chickpeas and diced potatoes.

Alu dum: potato curry.

Bharta: aubergines, onions and tomatoes roasted in wood fire.

Bhujias: dry fried vegetables.

Chana: spiced chickpeas, served with a nan.

Sarson da saag: vegetables in mustard leaves with butter.

Paneer: very thick soft white cheese.

Chholia te paneer: chickpeas and fried cheese dices.

Mattar paneer: cheese and peas in a sauce.

Palak paneer: cheese and cooked in a spinach paste

Thālis: the term "thāli" originates from a round metal tray with compartments. In certain rural areas, these trays can be replaced with banana tree leaves. For example, it is possible to have three dishes containing rice, yoghurt and a vegetable curry, served with pickles, chāpatīs, and pappadams.

Lentils

Dāl: a generic term for the many kinds of lentils commonly eaten in the country. Their high content in proteins and mineral salts allows a well-balanced vegetarian diet.

Dhal makhani: lentils in cream.

Raita: yoghurt and vegetables, normally cucumber .

Ghī: Main greasy substance in the cuisine of North India and used since the vedic era. It is a clarified butter whose water and impurities have been removed by heating and decantation.

Mithāī (sweets): a generic term to name several varieties of confectionery products Indians are very fond of. They are usually milk based.

Barfī: small cakes in the shape of rhombuses or squares, prepared with thickened milk, sugar and almonds (barfī bādām) or pistachios (barfī pistā). They can be covered with a very fine edible silvery sheet.

Firni: cream of rice with almonds, grapes and pistachios.

Gulāb jāmun: fried balls of flour and cream soaked in sugar syrup flavoured with rosewater and cardamom.

Halvā: mixture cooked in a greasy substance until a thick paste is obtained, sūjī halvā, semolina cake garnished with raisins and almonds, gājar halvā (carrot halvā), kelā halvā (bananas halvā).

Jalebī: spiral fritters of a yellow-orange colour. They are made of a fried  and crusty paste and are filled with sugar 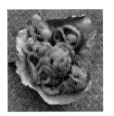 or honey syrup scented with rosewater.

Khīr: creamy sweetened rice lengthily cooked in milk with cardamom, rasins and sometimes saffron, pistachios, almonds and rosewater, generally prepared for religious festivals.

Kulfī: Indian dairy ice cream. It is a solid ice cream, not beaten and gelatine-free, granular, filled with small pieces of cream, pistachios and almonds. It is made with starch, Maizena or arrowroot scented with rosewater or kewrā. Laddū: balls containing semolina or chickpea flour cooked with ghī, sweetened and scented with cardamom. Very popular, the laddūs are offered to the divinity and to the participants in religious festivals.

Rasgullā: kinds of spongy ball made of soft white cheese (made with hand-curdled milk) and semolina cooked in scented sugar syrup.

Lassi: very popular refreshing soft drink prepared with curdled milk beaten in cold water. It can be drunk salted and slightly peppered or sweetened and scented with the rosewater, either mixed with banana or coconut.

Dahi (yoghurt): It alleviates the heat of spices during the meal, it is eaten as a dessert.

Fruits: They are often consumed cut in quarters, mixed together, and sometimes sprinkled with grey salt. The mangos (ām) are a fresh relief during the hot season. They are small and slightly sour, big and sweet, yellow or green. The banana (kelā) can be consumed throughout the year. The lemon (nimbū) enhances the taste of many dishes and it is used to make refreshing soft drinks (nimbū pānī). Guavas (amrūd), pomegranates (anār), papayas (papītā), melons, watermelons, pineapple, litchis abound on the markets depending on the season. But one also finds apples, pears, peaches, plums, apricots and figs, which are fruits, brought in by the various foreign influences. The cold season is favourable to the

tangerine of which the most scented ones come from the area of Kānpur (Uttar Pradesh). The coconut decorates the culinary dishes but it is also a symbol of fecundity. It is used as an offering in the temples. The Indians also eat lots of dried fruits (mevā) added to the dishes of the feast days: almonds, peanuts, dates, cashew nuts, pistachios and raisins being the most common ones.

Spices: one of the most remarkable features of the Indian cuisine is its art in the use of spices, whose variety is immense. They have well known medicinal properties. They help digestion and stimulate an appetite that languishes in the hot climate. The garam masālā is a mixture of various spices added to a dish at the end of the cooking process (mixture of pepper, cumin and cardamom, cinnamon, cloves). It varies from one area, or even from one family to another, secretly kept recipes are transmitted from mother to daughter or daughter-in-law.

Cardamom (Haychi): There are a number of varieties, one is large and black and another one is small and green, one is sweetened, the other bitter. They are often blended in the garam masālā. The ground pods from the green variety are used for the biryani and the polaos.

Clove (Laung): They are the dried floral buds of the clove tree. They are one of the fundamental components of the garam an masālā d are used in curries.

Coriander (Dhania): Plant of the umbelliferae family, whose leaves are very odorous. Its seeds (seeds of coriander) are used in the making of the curries.

Cumin (Zeera and Shah Zeera): They are the seeds from two different umbelliferae, Zeera, with a grey-yellowish seed, and the brown-black seeded Zeera Shah. Both are used depending on the dishes. They are found in the garam massala used for vegetables, the pulaos and some chutney dishes.

Curcuma (Haldi or Turmeric): It is a powder obtained by the reduction of a rhizome initially cooked with water and then dried. This powder (often known under the name of "Bourbon saffron") gives a strong yellow colour to the dishes.

Fenugreek (Ethi): The Indians are very fond of this plant's leaves (which look like clover leaves) and eat them with vegetables. The seeds, yellow-brown, are used in the making of some curries.

Ginger (Addu or Adrak): This rhizome is sold "in fingers", the "three-fingers" being the best quality. It is used ground as a curry ingredient.

Peppers (Lalmirchi or Mirchi): They are small strong peppers, green or red, used fresh or dried and in powder for the curries and the chutneys. Finely chopped, they are added to the green curries.

Saffron (Kesar): The Indians use the saffron-filaments, i.e. the not-ground stigmas of the flower. They crush them and then infuse them over 10 min in a hot liquid—water or milk—before mixing them with the desired preparation. Very commonly used in the biryani, the pulaos or the desserts and biscuits.

Rosewater: It is a sort of diluted essence, extracted via a steaming process. It is essential in certain dishes, and is measured with a teaspoon. It often scents the lassi.

Pān (betel leaves and nuts)

By the 16th century, the trading of betel leaves and areca nuts had become the greatest source of income of the rajahs, and the "carrier of the betel bag" was one of the highest ranked officials of the court. Nowadays, the betel still prevails in the Indian way of life, and its consumption is particularly liked in Kāshī. It is impossible to walk around without coming across uncountable stalls. One goes to the "pān-walla" as soon as there is a moment of respite. It is difficult to understand what people

are trying to say while keeping in their mouths the odd mixture blended with their own saliva. Their lips are red like a vampire after his meal. But this habit is so solidly rooted, that there are men able to hold long conversations while trying to keep in their mouths the precious mixture. Others will reduce their words to some rumbling noises. Comes the need, they spit the reddish liquid wherever possible and the streets and the walls of the old city are covered with them.

The betel leaf used to make this is a kind of climbing pepper plant, (climbing Piper betel), whose leaf has stimulant and astringent properties. It is used to wrap areca nuts (of the betel nut palm), from which the cachou is extracted. Slaked lime is added (essentially calcium hydroxide), often mixed with tobacco and other ingredients and aromatic agents such as camphor, aniseed, cardamom, nutmeg, clove, saffron, musk, coconut, fennel, ambergris or Indian saffron. Then, the chew is folded four times and closed up with a clove.

Chewing pān all day long gives men a sense of well being and gets them a little excited. It has stimulant and digestive properties, relieves hunger, stimulates a strong salivation and softens the breath. But it should be said that it is above all a cultural practice, which, however, is the main cause of mouth cancer. The consumption of areca nut is very high in India: 200,000 tons per annum.

Thandāī bhāng

The thandāī bhāng (pronounced tunde) would be a deformation of the American word sundae, a kind of milk shake. It is a mixture of fruits and crushed cashew nuts

mixed with bhāng. The bhāng is a kneaded paste made with water and fresh ganja leaves, an Indian cannabis well known for its narcotic effects and cultivated in the north of India and in Nepal. Although the legislation is severe as far as the drug is concerned, it is possible to find shops of bhāng in Kāshī, which are authorized by the government. Not far from the crossroads of Godauliā, the shop of the Baba thandāī is a cramped room, with its walls painted in a strong orange tone, decorated with religious motifs. At the entrance, sitting crosslegged on a small platform, a man cashes in the

orders. In front of him, an enormous ball of bhāng rests in a dish leant against a bronze cobra. Inside, benches surround a coffee table where the drinks are served. Large

milk glasses yellowed by spices and dry fruits goes with the consumption of bhāng. In the meantime, a man mixes the bhāng. He takes a small ball of the

soft and green paste with his fingertips and then places it in the client's hand. One ingurgitates it and then swallows a gulp of thandāī. A father comes in, carrying his child in his arms. Another person waits for his mixture to be prepared. Well wrapped in a plastic bag, he takes it with him, and as the most normal thing in the world, he returns to his daily occupations.

Sometimes Bhāng is more widely consumed during certain religious festivals, (Holī or Shivarātri). The ascetics (sādhus) are traditionally big consumers of bhāng, ganja or hash that can be smoked, chewed or mixed in different ways (cakes or drinks).

AROUND THE AREA

THE OPPOSITE BANK

The opposite bank is intriguing. Maghar. It is where the sun rises each morning in the hollow crescent shaped by the Ganges. So, our curiosity is excited by this large strip of white sand, this kind of "No-man' s land" animated by remote silhouettes. This sandy tongue attracts and scares at the same time because, as any common Banārsī will tell you, to die on the other bank means

to reincarnate as an ass, and to hear them, that really is not good for karma. It is thus necessary to take a boat, not only to take a look at the ghāts, but mainly to satisfy this curiosity. While disembarking, yo will see small gatherings there. Ablutions are made, but one also stops at the chāi shop to be refreshed and crunch on some biscuits there. Far away, a white horse gallops towards the horizon. Some children play their favourite sport under the sun, cricket, while a family have a picnic on the sand. In the azure sky, eagles mix with the multicoloured kites (patang) while you cross this long white strip. Walking

on the sand, you will find tiny white shells that the river water covers every monsoon. Away from the water boundaries, vegetation prevails once more. Laboriously, farmers try to extract from this soil even the tiniest harvests they can, by irrigating it. Men carry enormous milk cans on their heads. A bicycle waits against the well for its owner to come and pick it up. A hut is used as a shop; an old man sitting cross-legged waits for the rare customers to arrive. The path opens up to a modest village. Men beat the rice, children soak themselves in water, and a man rinses his placid buffaloes under the nonchalant glance of a dromedary. In front of a house, a woman filters the grain in a sieve. Very close to the agitation of the ghāts, there is suddenly the deep rural India, a very different way of life to the one in Kāshī, a dramatic change of scenery.

RĀMNAGAR

Rāmnagar is a small city located to the south-east of Kāshī five km away (by boat) on the opposite bank of the Ganges (fourteen km by road). It is a nice little jour-

ney to be made by boat (one hour to get there, one hour to return). It is located at the bottom of a pontoon bridge crossing over the Ganges. It is especially well known for the palace of the Mahārāja of Kāshī, which majestically overlooks the Ganges. On the way, there is the most famous lassis store in the surroundings. The palace, which includes a museum, was built in 1750, for the Mahārāja of Banāras whose dynasty belongs to the caste of the Bhūmihar Brahmans. You can find one of the manuscripts written by the poet Tulsī Dās's, a collection of antique cars, palanquins, elephant saddles (howdah), fire weapons, knives, ceremonial period costumes, objects finely carved in ivory, etc., there. One finds also a large clock,

which indicates the year, the month, the week, the day, the time, but also the configuration of the planets, the sun and the moon. This clock is a wonder of precision. It was made by a clockmaker of the Banāras State in 1872. There are also two small temples dedicated to Shiva. One of them, the Temple of Vyāsheshvara has a lingam that was in-

stalled here by the wise man Vyāsa, the legendary transcriber of the Veda.

Every year in Rāmnagar, during the 31 days between September and the beginning of October, there are performances of the Rām Līlā, the epic from Rāmcharitmānas, recounting the story of Rāma. It was written in Hindi by the poet from Kāshī, Tulsī Dās. This very popular event attracts more than 10,000 spectators each day and on the last performance, more than 50,000.

Not far from there, 2.5 km North-East from the fort, there is the splendid temple dedicated to Durgā, called Sumera Devī, which dates back from 1770.

SĀRNĀTH

"This places is matchless, perfectly calm, contemplating, always frequented by deer. In this most beautiful of parks, whose name was given by the sages, I will turn the holy Wheel".

Voice of the Buddha.

After six years of asceticism and renunciation, the Buddha achieves "the Illumination" (realisation) in Bodhgayā. He discovers that the way to follow is the "Middle Way", in between extreme asceticism and the profusion of pleasures. He then decided to find in Kāshī his former companions who had left him. So at

dawn he entered the Holy City. He gave alms, bathed in the Ganges, had a meal and moved on towards Rishipatana, Mrigadāya, the old names for Sārnāth.

This is a place located ten kilo-metres to the north of Kāshī. It is here that Siddhārtha Gautama pronounced his first sermon, 2,500 years ago in the "Deer" Park in front of his first five disciples (this sermon is called Dharmachakrapravartana, or First Spin of the Wheel of Dharma). The issue addressed in this First spin of the Wheel of Dharma was the Four Noble Truths which reveal the existence of suffering and dissatisfaction in our lives and shows us that the source of all problems is to be found in our mind-devouring attachment to objects and people. He spent the whole monsoon season preaching in Sārnāth, sheltered

from the rain, in a simple hut: the Mulagandhakuti Vihara, where he stayed during his numerous visits to Sārnāth. His first sixty disciples formed the "Sangha". They were in charge of spreading the teachings of Buddha: the Dharma.

Sārnāth became a significant Buddhist centre. The local rājas and the wealthy merchants based in Kāshī

largely contributed to the blossoming of Buddhism. In the 3rd century Sārnāth had become a significant arts centre which reached its apogee during the Gupta period (from the 4th to the 6th century). At the time of his visit to Sārnāth, during the rule of Chandragupta II, Fa-Hsien the Chinese pilgrim dis-covered four stūpas and two monasteries there. In the 7th century, Xuan Zhuang counted 30 monasteries and 3,000 monks.

Then, under the Pāla dynasty, the site continued to thrive before suffering, in 1026, the attacks of the Afghan plunderer Mahmūd of Ghaznī during one of his seventeen raids in the north of India.

Dharmachakrajina Vihāra is the last big monastery erected on the site. This construction was sponsored by the Rājā of Banāras Govinda-chandra's (of the dynasty of Gāhadavāla) wife Kumardevi, who reigned from 1114 to 1154.

Then the site was destroyed by the sultan of Delhi Qutb-ud-din Aibek in 1194, thus triggering the beginning of the almost complete disappearance of Buddhism in India. Over six centuries, the site was completely abandoned, until 1794, when Jagat Singh retrieved bricks from Dharmarājika Stūpa to erect new constructions.

In 1798, Jonathan Duncan, reintroduced Sārnāth which, following the discovery of Jagat Singh, would become an excavation site. Colonel C. Mackenzie, major Kittoe, Gertel, C Horne, Sir John Marshall, Hargreaves, Daya Ram Sahni found many significant items during their several excavations.

The Buddhist Singhalese, Anagarika Dharmapala, began the revival and the restoration of the Sārnāth monuments. He is the initiator of the construction of Mulagandhakuti Vihāra (a Buddhist temple built in 1931).

All the ancient buildings of Sārnāth were ransacked by the Muslims. The ruins include:

The Dhāmek Stūpa, whose structure dates from 2nd and 3rd century, is a cylindrical building remade and enlarged in 7th century. Built with bricks, it is still today more than 33 meters high and has a diameter of only thirty meters. It is decorated with friezes and is carved with recesses in the purest Gupta style. Its base is built out of stone. And many pilgrims come here to meditate.

Dharmarājika Stūpa is one of the rare stūpas dating from the time of Ashoka. But only the foundations remain since its looting by Jagat Singh.

The ruins of Mulagandhakuti Vihāra show the place where the Buddha spent his first monsoon.

Chaukhandī Stūpa was built, according to the tradition, at the very place where the Buddha met his

five disciples. Akbar ordered the erection of an octagonal tower in memory of his father Humāyūn.

The pillar of Ashoka, brought to ruins a long time ago, is, however, still standing. The capitol with the lions is the country's emblem today. It is exhibited in the archaeological museum run by the Archaeological Survey of India.

A pīpal tree (ficus religiosa) is venerated with much devotion. It was planted by Anagarika Dharmapala, from a shoot of the Bodhgayā tree.

Today, this park is a haven of peace where lovers like to stroll-in this pastoral environment full of historical surroundings. Pilgrims from all over the world come here to pray, as this is a particularly important place for the Buddhists.

GHĀTS

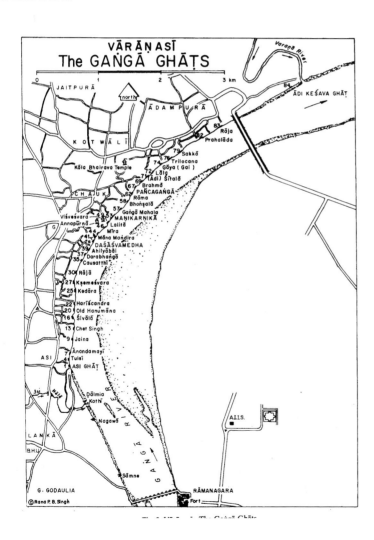

The ghāts are the steps, which lead to the waters of the Ganges and allows people to immerse. The ghāts of Kāshī stretch over more than seven kilometres on the western bank of the Ganges, drawing a big crescent. There are eighty-four of them along the Ganges's course, and each ghat has its own history, its own identity and a particular significance.

1. ASI GHĀT

Asi ghāt is an important ghat of Vārānasī. It constitutes traditionally the southern end of the city. Numerous references to this ghat are found in literature, particulaly in the Matsya Purāna, Kūrma Purāna, Padma Purāna and Kāshī khanda. According to a legend, it is here that the goddess Durgā had thrown her sword after killing the demon Shumbha-Nishumbha. When the sword (Khadga) fell, it caused a big stream to flow from that place, known as the river Asi. The Asi ghāt is located at the confluence between the rivers Gangā and the Asi. The Followers of Hindu religions make their sacred dip here, particularly in Chaitya (March/April) and Māgha (Jan/Feb) or during a solar or lunar eclipse. Asi ghāt is one of the five most important Tīrtha. (The Panchathirthī are: Asi,

255

Dashāshvamedha, Ādi Keshava, Panchagangā and Manikarnikā). A Tīrtha is a crossroads where the pilgrims have to take a holy dip.

2. GANGĀ MAHĀL GHĀT (I):

Gangā Mahāl ghāt is named after a building erected by the Mahārāja of Banāras at the northern end of the Asi ghāt (in 1830).

3. RIVAN GHĀT:

The Rivan ghāt is an extended part of the Asi ghāt and its building was carried out by Lala Mishir, a purohit (priest) of the King Ranjit Singh of Punjāb. It was know as the Lala Mishir ghāt. But in 1879, it was bought by the Mahārāja of Rivan. In the later half of the 20th century, the Mahārāja Rivan donated this building to the Banāras Hindu University.

4. TULSĪ GHĀT:

It is named after the great poet Tulsī (1547-1622 A.D.) who wrote the Rāmcharitmānas. It was know before as Lolārka ghāt. This ghāt is linked to a number of important activities such as the bathing of Lolārka kund (to get sons and have a long life), to cure leprosy. During the Hindu lunar month of Kārttika (Oct/Nov), the Krishna līlā (legend of Krishna) is also performed here in a big ceremony. Here, music concerts, wrestling, and spiritual speeches take place regularly.

5. BHADAINI GHĀT:

Since 1907, it has a huge pumping system to supply water for the whole city. This ghāt has a standing brick and stonewall. There is not any bathing or religious activities here.

6. JANAKI GHĀT:

In 1870, the Mahārānī Kunwar of Sursand from Bihār made this ghāt. Earlier on it was known as the "Nagamber ghāt". Religious ablutions take place here, since it is safe and clean.

7. ĀNANDAMAYĪ GHĀT:

In the past, it was know as the lmalia ghāt. In 1944, a woman who was a very respected and spiritual guru called Ānandamayī and bought this area from the British. She established an Āshram there. A number of religious activities take place here.

8. VACCHARĀJA GHĀT:

It was built by a merchant named Vaccharāja at the end of the 18th century and gave his name to it. It is believed that Suparshvanatha, (the seventh Tirthankar in the Jain's tradition) was born near this site. At present most of the Jain families live here. Along the up going stairs that go from the banks of the river Gangā to the streets, there are three niches dedicated to Shiva, Ganesh and the beautiful Gangā goddess (mūrti), riding on her vehicle, the crocodile. Occasional cultural events—bhajans and kirtans—are presented here. It is a comfortable ghāt for local people to take baths and exercise.

9. JAIN GHĀT:

Before 1931, the Jain ghāt was part of the Vaccharāja ghāt. Later on, the Jain community made it into a ghāt and named it the Jain ghāt. On the southern part of the ghāt, the Jain communities bathe and perform their regular activities, whereas up north, the Mallah (boatman) families make the place look differently.

10. NISHAD GHĀT:

Up to the first half of 20th century, it was a part of the Prabhu ghāt. Now, a large number of boatmen with their small boats and nets can be seen here. The ghāt has one Nishad Rāj Temple that was, as a matter of fact, constructed by the boatmen families only a few years ago.

11. PRABHU GHĀT:

This ghāt was built in the early part of the 20th century by Nirmal Kumar of Bengal. Most of the boatmen families

live here. Normally, the laundry washers (dhobīs) clean their clothes here.

12. PANCHAKOTA GHĀT:

On the northern end of the Prabhu ghāt, a palatial building and a ghāt were constructed by the King of Panchakota (Bengal) at the end of the 19th century. From the ghāt, some thin stairs lead to the palatial building with its two temples.

13.CHET SINGH GHĀT:

It is a historical fortified ghāt. The place witnessed a fierce battle between the troops of Warren Hastings and Chet Singh's army in 1781. The fort and the ghāt have been taken from the British by the Mahārāja Prabhu Nārāyan Singh in the second half of the 19th century. Originally, this ghāt was known as Khirki ghāt. Now it has four sections known as Chet Singh, Niranjani, Nirvani and Shivālā.

This ghāt has three Temples dedicated to Shiva dating from the 18th century to the first half of the 20th century. It was, culturally, of a great significance. The famous Budhwa Mangal festival, a seven-day event, is still celebrated here. Due to the strong currents of the Gangā people avoid bathing here. This ghāt was renovated by the government in 1958.

14. NIRANJANI GHĀT:

This ghāt belongs to the nāga's (renouncing Saints) who established the Niranjani Akhārā in 1897. Originally it was a part of the Chet Singh ghat. Now there are four temples including pāduka (footprints) of Niranjani Mahārāja Durgā Gaurī Shankar and Gangā images (mūrti). People do not take baths here because the place has no religious relevance.

15. MAHĀNIRVANI GHĀT:

It is situated in the north end of the Nirvani ghāt. It is named after the Mahānirvani sect of the nāga Saints. The famous akhārā is located here. It has four small Shiva temples built by the Mahārāja of Nepal. The legend says that Acharya Kapil Muni lived here and that the Buddha took baths here.

16.SHIVĀLĀ GHĀT:

It has been an important ghāt in the past. In the middle of the nineteenth century, it got divided into several small ghāts. At present, there is a colossal building constructed by the Nepalese King Sanjay Vikram Shah ,in the 19th century , as well as a Shiva temple and a Brahmendra Math (monastery), established by

Kāshīrāj. Only some pilgrims and local inhabitants take baths here. One of Mother Teresa's homes is situated here.

17. GULARIA GHĀT:

This ghāt was named after a huge Gular tree, which is not there anymore. It was built by Lalooji Agrawal. Debris from old houses are scattered on top of the stairs.

18. DANDI GHĀT:

It was made by Lalooji Agrawal. This ghāt got this name because of the ascetics and the sage Dandi who held a stick in their hand. This ghāt is quite clean and worth taking a bath in.

19. HANUMĀN GHĀT:

The temple dedicated to Hanumān gave its name to the ghāt. The ancient name of this ghāt was Rāmeshvaram ghāt, established by the lord Rāma himself. Many Vairagi ascetics live in the temple. The neighbourhood is inhabited mainly by South Indians.

20. PRACHINA (OLD) HANUMĀNAN GHĀT:

Both of the above (no 19 and no 20) ghāts were built by Mahant Hariharnath in 1825. This ghāt had an affinity with the great bhakti saint Valabha (1479-1531), who developed the philosophical foundations for a great resurgence of the Krishna bhakti. His birthday is celebrated during the month of Vaishākha (April-May). The temple of Rāma consists of five Shiva Lingams named after Rāma (Rāmeshvara), his two brothers (Lakshmansvara and Bhāratsvarar), his wife (Sitesvara) and his monkey-servant (Hanumāndisvara).

21. KARNATAKA GHĀT:

This ghat was built by the State of Mysore (now known as Karnataka) in the early twentieth century (1910). There is a shrine of Rūrū ("the Dog") Bhairava, one of the eight Bhairavas protecting the city in eight directions.

22. HARISHCHANDRA GHĀT:

This ghāt is named after the mythological King Harishchandra, who once worked here at the cremation sites for the preservation of truth and charity. In the end the Gods re-warded him and gave him back his "effects" and resurrected his dead son. This is one of the two cremation ghāts. In 1986-1987 an electric  crematorium was opened here, although the funeral wooden pyres continued. At the top of the temple there are images, (mūrti) of Harischandrsvara, Rohitesvara, Ādi Manikarnikeshvara and Vrddha Kedara. In 1740, Nārāyana Dixit Peshva, a religious guru, renovated this ghāt.

23. LALI GHĀT:

This ghat was built in 1778 by the Rāja of Banāras. The temples are in the high sector: Lambodara Cintamani and Jyestha Vinaykas, Kirateshvara, Jayanta Siva Lingam and Maha Lakshmī. Laundry men (dhobīs) are prominent in this ghat.

24. VIJAYANAGARAM GHĀT:

This ghāt was made in 1890 by the Vijayanagaram State, the kingdom in South India. At the top of it, there is the Svami Karapatri Āshram. Close to this building we find the shrines of Nilakantha and Nispapeshvara.

25.KEDĀRA GHĀT:

This is the site of Haramapapa Tīrtha. Above it, there is the temple of Kedāreshvara, the patron deity of the south-ern sacred segment. The attached shrines and holy sites

are: Tarakesvara, Gaurī Khunda and Vitanka Nrsimha. In the late sixteenth century Kumārasvami, a devotee of Dattātreya, built a monastery attached to the Kedāreshvara temple.

26. CHAUKI GHĀT:

This ghat is famous for the huge pīpal (ficus religiosa) tree at the top of the steps, which shelters a great array of stone figures of snakes, nāgas. Havell described this ghat: "under a fine old pīpala-tree, there is a small shrine and a great number of old carved stones, some of snakes twined together like Mercuty's caduceus, with some fine figurines sculpted on the platform surrounding the tree. They are probably remains of the early Buddhist period". The shrine of Rukmangeshvara is close to this tree, a little further away, the Nāga Kupa ("Snake Well"). During the festival to honour the snake, the Nāga Panchamī, during Shrāvana (July–August), these shrines are especially worshipped. This ghat was built in 1790.

27. KSHEMESHVARA GHĀT:

Its old name was Nala ghat, and was built in the early eighteenth century. The followers of Kumaraswami built a monastery in 1962 at the upper side of the steps. The shrines of Kesemesvara and Ksemaka Gana are at the top of the steps. The neighbourhood is mainly inhabited by Bengali residents.

28. MANASAROVARA GHĀT:

At the top of this ghat there is a sacred pond. It is a replica of the famous holy lake with the same name in Tibet. This ghat was built by the Rāja Mana Singh of Jaipur in 1585, and was rebuilt in 1805. The shrines of Rāma, Lakshmana, and Dattātreya are in the surroundings.

29. NĀRADA GHĀT:

The old name of this ghat is the Kuvai ghat. It was built by Dattātreya Swami, the head of a monastery, in 1788. The four important images (mūrti) in the upper side are Nāradeshvara, Atrisvara, Vasukisvara and Dattātreyeshvara. This ghat is attached to Nāradeshvara, a lingam established by the mythical sage Nārada.

30. RĀJA GHĀT:

Formerly known as the Amrita Rao ghat, it was firstly made by the first Maratha chief Bajirao Balaji in 1720. It was rebuilt with stone slabs by Amrita Rao (1780-1807). At the top of the stone steps there are four temples: Amritesvara, Vinayakesvara, Nayanesvara and Gangesvara and four auxiliary shrines, as well as Prabhasa Tīrtha, renovated in 1780.

31. KHORI GHĀT:

Also known as the Gangā Mahāla ghat, it was erected in the late nineteenth century by Kavindra Nārāyana Singh. Above it, there are five magnificent temples.

32. PANDA GHĀT:

In 1805, this ghat was built in honour of a famous wrestler who established a wrestling site (akhārā) there. His name was Babua Pande. The shrine of Somesvara exists close by to it. In its vicinity lies the old site of Prabhasa Tīrtha.

33. SARVESHVARA GHĀT:

This ghāt was erected under the sponsorship of Mathura Pandey in the late eighteenth century. The Gangā Keshava Tīrtha and Sarveshvara image (mūrti) are near the ghāt.

34 DIGPATIA GHĀT:

This one was erected in 1830 by the Rāja of Digpatia (Bengāl). The beautiful building along the ghāt is now known as "Kāshī Āshram".

35. CHAUSATTHĪ GHĀT:

The number sixty-four (Chausatha) symbolises the directions and the mother-goddesses with their servant-goddesses. There are of course- other interpretations too. This ghāt had the privilege to receive a great Sanskrit scholar, Madhusudana Sarasvatī (1540-1623). Above the ghāt there is the temple of Chausatthī Devī, but only sixty images (mūrti) of the yoginī are found there, the last four are located in various places. In 1670, the King of Udaipur (Rājasthān) renovated this ghāt. Many pilgrims visit the yogini temple and take ritual baths at this ghāt. On the evening of Holī (a colourful festival) in the

month of Chaitra (March-April), a ritual homage is celebrated at the ghāt.

36. RANA MAHĀLA GHĀT:

Actually, this is an extended part of the previous ghāt, and was also erected by the King of Udaipur in 1670. At the top there is the Vakratunda Vināyaka's shrine.

37. DARBHANGA GHĀT:

In 1915 the King of Darbhanga (Bihār) erected simultaneously two buildings: the magnificent building along the ghāt and a big Shiva temple in the Nilakantha area. The building along the ghāt shows a massive Greek pillars style. The shrine of Kukutesvara is found at the top.

38. MUNSHI GHĀT:

The ghāt was built as an extended part of the Darbhanga ghāt, by Sridhar Nārāyan Munshi, a finance minister in the State of Darbhanga, in 1912. After his death in 1924, this ghāt was named in his honour.

39. AHILYĀBĀĪ GHĀT:

In 1778, Queen Ahilyābāī Holkar of Indore built this ghāt at the same spot where the old site for the Kevelyagiri ghāt had been. For the first time, a name of a person was given to the ghāt. She was also responsible for the reconstruction of the Visveshvara temple as it is today, in 1777.

40. SHĪTALĀ GHĀT:

In 1740, Nārāyana Dixit the master of Bajirao Peshva built this ghāt. It is in actual fact the southern extension of the Dashāshvamedha ghāt. Dashāshvamedha Tīrtha and images (mūrti) of Dashāsvamedhesvara as well as Dashāshareshvara are found here. This ghāt is named after the famous temple that bears the same name. On the months of Chaitra (March-April), Vaishākha (April-May), Jyeshtha (May-June), Āshādha (June-July) and Āshvina (Sept -Oct), people celebrate the festival of Shītalā Asthami. Another important celebration at this ghāt is the special worship that follows the weddings. The couples and the close relatives come here for the Gangā's worship ritual and then attend the rituals in the Shītalā temple.

41. DASHĀSHVAMEDHA GHĀT:

This is the busiest, the most popular and the most ancient ghāt. According to the myth of Divodāsa, the Lord Brahmā ("the Creator" in the Hindu

Prinsep

trinity of gods) performed the ten-horses sacrifice (dasā-asvamedha) at this site. Other historical sources say that it was at this site that Bhara Shiva Nagas (from the Hindu dynasty of the third century), carried out the sacrifice. The Kāshī khanda records many verses describing the glory of this ghāt. The temple of Sulatankesvara, Brahmesvara, Varahesvara, Abhaya Vināyaka, the Gangā ("goddess"), and Bandi Devī are at the top of the ghāt. These shrines are linked to several important pilgrimage journeys. The southern part of the ghāt was built in 1748 by Balaji Bajirao, and later in 1774 by Ahilyā Bāī Holkar.

42. PRAYĀGA GHĀT:

This ghāt together with the shrine of the Prayāgageshvara recalls, in Vārānasī, the existence of the town called

Prayāga—also known as Allāhābād. Prayāga commonly called "Tīrtharāja" (king of Tīrtha), Prayāga is at the confluence of the Gangā, the Yamunā and the invisible Sarasvatī rivers. It is traditionally believed that doing rituals and having sacred baths here provide exactly the same religious merits as doing it in Prayāga (80 km away in the west). The merits of this area are glorified in the Kāshī Khanda. The temple and the ghāt areas were reconstructed by the Queen of the Digpatia state (West Bengal). Over the whole month of Magha (Jan-Feb) devotees bathe more specifically at this site.

43. RĀJENDRA PRASAD GHĀT:

In 1979, this ghāt was renamed, in memory and honour of the first president of India (1950-1962), Rājendra Prasad (1884-1963), and erected by the Municipal Corporation of Vārānasī. In actual fact, this ghāt was the northern extension of the Dashāsvamedha ghāt. And until the end of the nineteenth century a stone horse statue was at the ghāt, witnessing the "ten-horses sacrifices" performed by Bhara Shiva Nagas. This is the origin of the name "Ghoda ghāt" ("Horse ghāt"). The myth says that the servants of Bhara Shiva Nagas took baths here.

44. MĀN MANDIRA GHĀT:

The old name of this ghāt was Someshvara, but in 1585 when King Savai Mān Singh (from Amber in Rājasthān), erected his palace this ghāt was named after him. This ghāt is known primarily for its magnificent building, with finely carved windows. At the top, there is a Hindu Observatory built by Savi Jai Singh II (1686-1743) in 1710. Other places where he built such observatories are Jaipur, Delhi, Mathura and Ujjain. Under the direction of the poet-astrologer and minister, Jagannātha, the King came to observe the skies on several occasions in 1710-1737. There are four main astronomical instruments there and renovations were made in 1850 then again in

Prinsep

1912, under the patronage of the King of Jaipur. The nearby shrines at the top of the ghat are the ojnes of Somesvara, Dalabhesvara, Ramesvara and Sthuladanta Vinayaka.

The Prabhasa Tirtha is located at the banks of the river. During Holī, the annual festival of colours takes place on the last day of Phālguna (Feb-March) people celebrate at the Dalabhesvara's shrine.

45. TRIPURA BHAIRAVĪ GHĀT:

This ghat is named after the goddess Tripura Bhairavī, whose shrine and image (mūrti) are also here. Another important shrine is Varahi, one of the nine mother-goddesses. At the end of the eighteenth century the King of Banāras and the President Māyānanda Giri sponsored the construction of this ghat.

46. MĪR GHĀT:

This ghat represents two old sites of Jarasandhesvara and Vrdhaditya, which were converted by the Muslim Commander Mīr Rustam Ali in 1735. Currently, in honour to these two shrines, the pilgrims throw flowers and raw rice into the Gangā. The shrines and the images (mūrti) in the surroundings are Vrdhaditya, Asa Vināyaka, Yajna

Varahaand Visalaksi ("The Wide-Eyed", one of the 52 Sakti-pithas of goddesses). Another important site is Dharma Kūpa consisting of a holy well surrounded by five temples, and also the Divodāseshvara lingam. The temple of Dharmesha is linked to the myth of Yama's (Lord of Death)— that sets the fate of the dead everywhere on earth, except in Kāshī.

Because of the presence of the low castes ("The Untouchables") the Vishvanātha temple and the Vishveshvara's became impure, so Swami Karapatri-Ji, a very conservative Brahmin, established the "New Vishvanātha Temple" in 1956 at top of the ghat. On the steps, under a pipal tree, the ritual of water pouring takes place, to honour the ancestors.

47. PHUTA/ NAYA GHĀT:

This was the old site for the Yajnesvara ghat and was built by Svami Maheshvarananda in the middle years of the nineteenth century. Near the river lies the Visala Gaja Tīrtha.

48. NEPĀLĪ GHĀT:

Havell described this ghat: "Recessed in a stone embankment, and completely covered by the river in the rainy season, there is the pretty little shrine of Gaṅgā. Gaṅgā is represented as a female figure seated on a crocodile. Overhanging it, a staircase leads to the Nepalese temple, a very picturesque building -also called the Kathwala temple half-hidden by a magnificent tamarind and pīpal trees. It is made mainly of wood and brick. The double storied roof, with great projecting eaves supported by brackets, is typical of the architecture of Nepal and of other sub-Himalayan districts".

The temple was patronised by the Nepalese. The workers who carved this temple were brought from Nepal. The wood used in the temple is also found in Nepal. The speciality of this wood is that termites cannot eat it. The area is mainly inhabited by Nepalese (Nepālī Khapra).

49 LALITĀ GHĀT:

This ghāt is named after the famous goddess Lalitā in Kāshī and is also worshipped in Prayāga (Allāhābād). The well-known lingam of Gaṅgā Keshava and the shrines from Gaṅgātitya, Kāshī Devī, Lalitā Devī and Ghagirath Tīrtha are related to this site. People believe that a glimpse of Lalitā Devī delivers the same merits as travelling over the entire world. As described earlier, at the top of the ghāt, close to the Nepālī ghāt, lies the Nepālī Temple built under the patronage of the king of Nepal. The lingam there is supposed to be the replica of the famous Pashupatishvara from Kathmandu. The temple has wooden carvings depicting erotic scenes, and all the four gateways and doors are fully decorated with geomagnetic architectural frames.

50. BAULI GHĀT:

The old name of this ghāt was Rāja Rājeshvari ghāt. It was erected in the beginning of the nineteenth century by a rich merchant, Babu Keshava Deva. In the nearby stream lies the Bramha Nāla Tīrtha.

51. JALASĀĪ GHĀT:

This ghāt is also called Jalasen ghāt. In actual fact it is one of the cremation ghāts. The name itself means "putting a dead body into the water", after a part of a ritual that takes place before the corpse is laid on the funeral pyre. The nearby building and the ghāt were built in the middle of the nineteenth century.

52. KHIRKI GHĀT:

The name of the ghāt literally means "the windows" (Khirki), from where the attendants can watch the cremations. Close to it, Baldeo Dasa Birla built a pilgrims resthouse in 1940. There are five Satī shrines under a pīpal tree.

53. MANIKARNIKĀ GHĀT:

Two ancient sacred waterfront sites make this ghāt: Sidha Vināyaka and Svargadvāra. It is commonly called "the great cremation ground"

Prinsep

(Mahāshmashāna). A myth recounts that Lord Shiva whispers the Tāraka mantra ("Prayer for the crossing") in the ears of the dead, therefore the representation of Shiva as Tārakeshvara, (the temple is at the ghāt), is appropriate whenever a Hindu dies. The name Manikarnikā comes from the earring that Shiva dropped here during her transcendental dance. Historical sources mention this site in the Gupta's inscriptions of the 4th century. This is the first ghāt erected by the two brother kings in 1302. It

was rebuilt and repaired in 1730 under the patronage of Bajirao, and, in 1791, Ahilyābāī rebuilt the entire ghāt. Again in 1872 repairs and renovations were undertaken. In the vicinity we find the shrines of Manikarnikeshvara (a little further away in the upper side of the lane), Maheshvara (an open air lingam at the ghāt) and Siddha and Manikarna Vināyakas. The temple of Manikarnikeshvara is accessible from the ghāt through an ascending lane in the south of the Kund.

There is also a sacred pond, Cakra Puskarini Kund ("Discus Lotus-Pool") and Vishnu's footprints: Carana pādukā. According to the puranic myth, the Cakra-Puskarini Kunda was there well before the Gangā arrived at the heels of Bhagiratha. For the benefit of the King of the Three Worlds, Bhagīratha brought the Gangā from Manikarnikā to the Shiva's Forest of Bliss ("Ānandavana"), and to Vishnu's Lotus Pool (Chakra-Puskarni Kund). Currently the Kund is surrounded by a cast-iron rail. Vishnu and Lakshmī's images (mūrti) are located in the small shrine inside the Kund on the western

wall. A series of 12 small niches containing Shiva lingams are also there. Along the holy route, and on the ghāt itself, there are the symbolic footprints of Vishnu (Carana pāduka), set in a circular marble slab. For 7,000 years Vishnu would have done tapas there, and through the centuries millions of Hindus have wetted it with the holy Gangā water and adorned it with flowers. It is considered to be the holiest place in the sacred City.

The place nearby this holy site is reserved for the cremation of very important people, such as the Mahārāja of Kāshī.

This ghāt area was famously known in the past as a cremation site. The promontory attached to the ghāt is used for rituals linked to anniversaries of deaths. In between the Jalasaī and the Manikarnikā ghāts there are fourteen Tīrtha, among them, Vishnu's, Bhavani's, Skanda's, Tāraka's, Avimuktesvara's and Pashupati's.

Overlooking the Manikarnikā ghāt, is the Shiva-Durgā temple of Rāja of Amethy (from Uttar Pradesh), built in 1850. It is different from the others in that it has five deep red spires and gilded pinnacles.

It is built on a terrace overlooking the river, and is accessible through one of these steep, staircases streets, leading from the ghāt up to the city. Climbing up a side staircase, you go under the Naubata Khana, where musicians are chanting prayers to the goddess with strange but not unpleasant accompaniments. On the right side of the entrance is a fine bronze lion of Durgā, and on the left Shiva's bull.

54. BAJIRAO GHĀT:

Bajirao Peshva built this ghāt in 1735; hence it is named after him. He also erected a palace. In actual fact the entire structure sunk several meters into the earth after its construction. Later in 1830, Queen Baijabai of Gwalior had it repaired and rebuilt. She also erected the colonnade around the Jnāna Vāpī well. At the top, there is the temple of Dattātreyeshvara, giving its name to the Dattātreya ghāt. Currently, it is considered to be part of the Scindhiā ghāt.

55. SCINDHIĀ GHĀT:

It was formerly known as the Vireshvara ghāt, because of the temple with the same name, located on its top. In 1780 Ahīlyabāī Holker of Indore built the ghāt. In 1829, the Queen Baijabai got it repaired and transformed. In 1937, Daulatarao Scindhiā built back the entire  ghāt. The shrines of Vsistha and Vamadeva, and Atmavireshvara are at the top. The Paravata Tīrtha lies in the nearby River Gangā.

56. SANKATHA GHĀT:

Its old name was Yameshvara ghāt, after the name of the shrine. At the top, in the lane, there are the temples of Yameshvara and Harischandreshvara that were the old cremation sites. Still now, during the Yama Dvitiya festival, devotees take their sacred baths. At the end of the

18th century, the King of Baroda built this ghat. But in 1825, Beniram Pandit's widow (known as "Panditain") and her nephews built this ghat and a structure for the temple of Sanktha Devī. At the top of the ghat, towards the city, there are the shrines of the Katyayini and Siddhesvari goddesses together with three Vināyakas: Harishchandra, Cintamani, Mitra and Vasukisvara. A new image (mūrti) of Santoshī Mātā ("Mother of Satisfaction") has also been built recently at the top. In between the Manikarnikā and the Scindhiā ghāts there are three water-Tīrtha: Uma, Sārasvata and Kamblasvetara.

57. GANGĀ MAHAL GHĀT (2):

There is another ghat with the same name. This one, in fact, is an old part of the Yameshvara ghat. The King of Gwalior built it at the beginning of the 19th century, and later on it was repaired and rebuilt by Govinda Bali Kiratankara.

58. BHONSALA GHĀT:

In 1780, king Maratha Bhonsala of Nagpur erected this ghat, and later on, in 1795, the temple of Lakhsmī Nārāyana and a square were also built. Two important shrines called Yameshvara and Yamaditya are nearby the palace.

59. NAYA GHĀT:

In the 1822's Prinsep's map, this ghat was named the Gularia ghat. It was probably constructed only a few years before that date.

60. GANESHA GHĀT:

This one was formerly known as the Agnishvara ghat after the Agni Tīrtha, the nearby river. Later on, the Peshva's Ganesha temple gave its name to this place. The important shrines at the top are the ones of Bhadresvara and Nagesa Vināyaka. Another important water-Tīrtha is Iksavaku Tīrtha. In the puranic texts this ghat is referred to as the Vighneshvara ghat. In the month of Bhādrapada (August/September) a special celebration is held there.

61. MEHTA GHĀT:

Formally this was part of the previous ghat, but following the construction of the V.S.Mehta hospital (1962), it is referred to with its new name. The Vārānasī Municipal Corporation made this ghat in 1960s. There are three Tīrtha along this ghat: Maitravaruna, Marutta and Iksavaku.

62. RĀMA GHĀT:

This name of this ghat 's originates from the Rāma Tīrtha and the shrine of Vira Rāmeshvara. Two other nearby water-Tīrthas are Kala Gangā and Tamra Varaha. The famous Vedic school (unique among the others of its kind) the Sanga Veda School, is situated not far from there. Rāma's birth is celebrated in the month of Chaitra (March-April) and the birth of Ganesha, in the month of Bhādrapada (August-September). The Rāma and Badarinārāyana shrines are located at the ghat.

63. JATARA GHĀT:

64. RĀJA GWALIAR GHĀT:

Both these ghāts, (Jatara ghāt and Rāja Gwaliar ghāt) and also the Rāma ghāt, were erected by the patronage of Madhorao Peshva in 1766. In fact, they are the two ends of the same ghāt.

65. MANGALĀ GAURĪ GHĀT:

This ghāt was built by Balaji Peshva-I in 1735, and therefore it is also known as the Bala ghāt. Later on, in 1807, Lakmana Bala from Gwalior repaired and renovated it. At the top of the ghāt, in the middle of the temple compound, images (mūrti) of Gabhastishvara, Mangalā Gaurī and Mangalā Vināyaka are found. Mangalā ("Auspiciousness") Gaurī is one of the nine motherly white Goddesses. At the ghāt, there are shrines with typically covered structures called Raghavendreshvara, and Kārttika Devī.

66. VENIMADHAVA GHĀT:

This is part of the Panchagangā ghāt, also known as the Vindu Madhava ghāt after the name of the famous temple built in the tenth century. The Vindu Madhava temple, which had been in ruins since 1496, was rebuilt by the Mahārāja of Amber in 1585 together with the Mān Mandira ghāt. But in 1669, the temple was demolished by Aurangzeb and replaced by a mosque. The image (mūrti) of Vindu has been re-installed in the upper floor of the Lakshmanabālā building and still attracts thousands of devotees and pilgrims for worship.

67. PANCHAGANGĀ GHĀT:

This is one of the five most sacred waterfront sites, and it is believed to be the confluence of five rivers: the Gangā, the Yamunā, the Sarasvatī and the two lost streams, the Kiranā and the Dūthapāpā. The merit and glory of this ghāt are described in an 11th century text and also in the Kāshī khanda. It was the residence of the great teacher of Vedanta, Rāmānanda (1400-1480), who was also the great reformist bhakti poet Kabīr's (1440-1518) guru. The Rāmānanda's monastery is still there. Tulsī (1532-1623) came to this ghāt, where he wrote the famous Vindu-patrika.

The ghāt was made of stone steps in 1580 by the finance secretary of the Mughal King Akbar. In 1735, Bajirao Peshva I, together with Sadasive Naik, rebuilt and repaired it. Again in 1775 renovations and repairs were undertaken by Sripatirao Peshva, and Pant Pririnidhi from Andhra. There are eight waterfront holy Tīrtha at the ghāt: Pīpalada, Vindu Makha, Mayukharka, Jnanahrda and Panchananda. There are two monasteries at the ghāt: Sri and Rāmānanda. At the ghāt, close to the riverfront, there are dozens of three-sided cubicle shrine rooms that open out onto the river. Some contains a lingam or an image (mūrti) used primarily for yogic exercises and meditation. Sherring has vividly described this ghat:

"The ghat is broad and deep, and exceedingly strong. Its stairs and turrets are all of stone, and from their great number, afford accommodation to a multitude of worshippers and bathers".

The Gangā āratī (oil lamps offering) is performed in honour to the Gangā with the sunrise and the sunset and it is the most attractive event of this ghat. The shrine of the goddess Gangā is also here. During the months of Vaishākha (April-May) and Kārttika (Oct-Nov.), devotees, mostly ladies, take morning sacred baths at this ghat. Special festivities and holy baths are take place on the Ganges's birthday. In the month of Kārttika (Oct-Nov.) the ghātiās (ghat priests) offer oil lamps to the ancestors. These lamps are placed in baskets held by big bamboo stands. There is a stone pillar with a thousand-stone socketed structure to keep the lamps alight during the full moon in the month of Kārttika.

The landmark of this area is the Alamgir mosque, which was built at the site of the late 11th century Vishnu temple. It was destroyed in the 15th century and re-made in 1585 by the King of Amber, but finally demolished and transformed into a mosque in 1673 by the Mughal emperor Aurangzeb.

68. DURGĀ GHĀT:

The name originates from the Brahmācharini Durgā temple. In 1772, Nārāyana Dixit, a guru from Peshvas, had purchased the land from the local fishermen resi-dents and built two ghāts: Durgā and Brahmā ghāts. Durgā was rebuilt and repaired in 1830 by Nana Phadanavisa whose building at the top of the ghāt is known as Phadanavisa Wada. At the ghāt, we find the Marakandeya and the Kharva Nrsimha Tīrthas, and there is also Kharva Nrsimha's shrine. With the full moon in the month of Kārttika, youngmen fight there to show their courage.

69. BRAHMĀ GHĀT:

This is named after the temples of Brahmā and Brahmeshvara. The other significant Tīrtha shrinse are Bhairava Tīrtha and Vindu Madhava. At the ghāt there are monasteries called Kāshī Matha Sansthana and Sudhindra Tīrtha Svami.

70. BUNDI PARKOTA GHĀT:

It was formerly known as the Rāja Mandira ghāt. In 1580, the King of Bundi, Rāja Surajana Hada made this ghāt. It was renovated in the middle of the nineteenth century. In its nearby areas we find the shrines of Sesa Madhava, Karnadity and Lakshmī Nrsimha.

71. (Ādi) SHĪTALĀ GHĀT:

This is an extended part of the preceding ghat, also made by Hada in 1580. Later on, in 1772, it was repaired and rebuilt by Nārāyana Dixit. This ghat is named after the old temple of Shītalā, known as "Badi" (older) Shītalā. The other goddess-shrines in the surroundings are: Nāgeshvarī Devī ("Snake Goddess") and Nārāyani.

Karanaditya. Tīrtha and Sankha Madhava are other holy places. Close to the site, there are also stones in memory of the Satīs. In the months of Chaitra, Vaishākha, Jyeshtha and Āshādha (from March to July) festivities take place in honour of the mother goddess.

72. LALA GHĀT:

This ghat was erected by a rich merchant in 1800, hence his name. As a part of this ghat in 1935, Baldeo Das Birla built a small ghat called Gopi Govinda, at the top of which there is a pilgrims' resthouse also built by him.

73. HANUMĀNGARHI GHĀT:

This was perhaps established in the end of the 19th century. It represents the famous site of Hanumāngarhi in Ayodhya (Rāma's birth place). Hanumān is the servant monkey of the Lord Rāma. The Gangā Akhārā (wrestling site), and a Satī-stone are also found on this ghat. Other shrines in the area are Gopi Govinda and Gopreksevara.

74. GAYĀ GHĀT:

In the 12th century, it was considered to be the southern boundary of the city. In the surrounding area there are still symbolic relics of that period, such as the Patana Darvaja. At the ghat there is a huge image (mūrti) of a cow (gaya/gai), symbolizing the Earth, this is why this

ghat is known as Gayā ghat. At the beginning of the 19th century, the ghat was constructed by Balabhai Sitole of Gwalior. At the top of the ghat, there are four images (mūrti): Bagesvari Devī, Nāgeshvarī Devī, ("Snake Goddess"), Mukarnirmalika Devī ("Pure-Faced Goddess") and Samhara Bhairava.

75.BADRI NAYARAN GHĀT:

This ghat was earlier known as Mahatha/Matha, or Balabhai ghat. Balabhai from Gwalior supported the construction of this ghat in the beginning of the 19th century. Later, the Municipal Corporation of Vārānasī had it repaired and renovated. The holy shrines linked to the site are Nāgeshvara Tīrtha, Nāgeshvara, Nāgesa Vināyaka and Nara-Nārāyana Keshava. The last shrine is originally at Badrinath, from where the name of the ghat originates: Badri (the site) and Nārāyana (the deity). With the full-moon day of Pausha (Dec-Jan.), a special festivity in the honour of Vishnu (in the avatar of Nara-Nārāyana) is celebrated. Also, in the month of Vaishākha (Apr-May) there is a holy bath ceremony.

76.TRILOCHANA GHĀT:

The name originates from the famous image (mūrti) of Shiva, Trilochana ("Three-Eyed"), whose lingam is known as Trilocaneshvara. The Kāshī Khanda and other contemporary books include many verses glorifying this ghat. Under the Gāhadāvala rule, in 1100, this ghat was a very popular site for sacred baths and rituals. Renovations and repairs were carried out by Nārāyana Dixit in 1772. Subsequently, circa 1795, Nathu Bala of Pune erected the ghat.

77. GOLA GHĀT:

Since the end of the 12th century, this site has been used as a river crossing point. However, after the opening of the bridge at the Rāja ghat in 1887, the site lost its relevance. References on the Pisegila Tīrtha (and on this ghat) are found in the Purānas. At the top we find the shrine of Burgu Keshava (Vishnu).

78. NANDESHVARA /NANDU GHĀT:

This ghat dates from the 20th century and was built by the locals. There is an Akhāra (wrestling site) bearing the same name there.

79. SAKKA GHĀT:

References on this ghat the Pranava Tīrtha could be found since the 18th century. Most of the ghat is occupied by washermen (dhobīs).

80. TELIANALA GHĀT:

From the end of the 18th century, it has been known as Hiranyagarbha Tīrtha, the ancient holy place. The legend says that the area was dominated by the oil pressing caste (Teli) that settled down at the banks of the stream (nala) hence its name.

81. NAYA/PHUTA GHĀT:

In medieval books this site is mentioned as Gopratara Tīrtha, with its holy waterfront site and its image (mūrti) of Gopratateshvara. During the 18th century, the ghat area was abandoned (Phuta), but it was later renovated. In 1940 Narsingh Jaipala Chainput-Bhabhua (Bihār) built this ghat.

82. PRAHLĀDA GHĀT:

It is named after Prahlāda, a great mythological devotee of Lord Vishnu. In the 11th and 12th centuries the Gāhadāvala inscriptions mentioned this ghat. It spreads over a longer area. In 1937 with the construction of a new Nishada ghat in the middle (where Satsanga Akhārā is), the ghat was divided into two parts in the south and in the north. In the southern part there are the shrines of Prahaladeshvara, Prahlāda Keshava, Vidara Narsimha, and Varada and Picindala Vināyakas. In the northern site we find Mahisasura Tīrtha, Svaralingesvara, Yajna Varaha and Sivaduti Devī. In the month of Vaishākha (April-May), a massive festival to honour Nrsimha ("Lion-Man" incarnation of Lord Vishnu) takes place in the temple of Prahaladesvara.

83. RĀJA GHĀT:

Up to 1887 this was a famous ghāt used to cross the river by boat. On the 1st January 1887, Lord Duffrin built a bridge and the ghat lost its importance as a ferry pier. The bridge was named Mālavīya Bridge in 1948 after the name of the Banāras Hindu University's founder, President Madan Mohan Mālavīya. In the Gāhadāvala inscriptions (1100) this ghāt is mentioned many times describing its glory and merits. There are four water Tīrtha linked to this ghāt: Sankhya, Uddalaka, Hayagriva and Nilagriva.

84. ĀDI KESHAVA GHĀT:

In the 12th century this ghāt was mentioned as the Vedeshvara ghat. It is supposed to be the oldest (Ādi) Lord Vishnu's site (Keshava). The temples-compound of Ādi Keshava has a pleasant rural aspect on the banks above the confluence of the Varanā and the Gangā rivers. According to the Purānas, it is one of the oldest holy sites in the city. It was the favourite holy site of the Gāhadāvala kings, as mentioned in the Gāhadāvala inscriptions. A great number of rituals in Vārānasī included the worship of Ādi Keshava or a dip in the Gangā, at the Varanā confluence. The ghāt was built in 1790 by a Divan of the Scindhiā State.

According to a famous legend, the five most sacred Tīrthas, called Panchatīrthī, (holy places) represent the body parts of the Lord: "Asi is the head, Dashāshvamedha is the chest, Manikarnikā is the navel, Panchagangā are the thighs, and Ādi Keshava are the feet" (Eck). This reminds us that Vishnu first placed his holy feet here, in Vārānasī. His footprints (Carana pāduka) in the Ādi Keshava temple symbolise this fact. The same footprints are also found at the Manikarnikā ghat.

Bathing at the confluence of the Varanā and the Gangā and paying a visit to Sangamesvara ("Lord of the Confluence") grants a special religious merit, as referred in the Linga Purāna:

"An excellent lingam has been installed by Brahmā at this confluence. It is known in the world as Sangameshvara. If a man shall become pure taking his bath at the confluence of the divine river and then worship Sangameshvara whence need he fear rebirth?".

The Sangameshvara lingam is located in temple attached to Ādi Keshava. Close to it we find the Brahmeshvara lingam (a four-sided lingam), believed to have been established by Brahmā ("The Creator").

Between Prahlāda and Ādi Keshava ghāt (from south to north) there are ten water-Tīrtha marking the bank: Sankha Madhava, Sasa, Lakshīminrsimha, Gopi Govinda, Vindara Nrsimha, Yajna Varaha, Mara-Nārāyana, Vāmana, Pranava and Dattātreyeshvara. And between the Ādi Keshava ghāt and the confluence of the Varanā, there are twelve water Tīrtha: Āditya Keshava, Ambarisa, Nārada, Garuda, Mahalakshmī, Padma, Gada, Cakra, Sankha, Ksirabdhi, Svetadvipa and Padodaka.

The birthday of Vāmana ("the Dwarf", 5th incarnation of Vishnu) is a massive celebration that takes place at the Ādi Keshava temple in the month of Bhādrapada (Aug-Sept).

BIBLIOGRAPHY:

Diana L. Eck: Banaras, City of light
Octavio Paz: Lueurs de l'Inde
Rana P.B. Singh and Pravin S.Rana: Banaras Region: A Spiritual and Cultural Guide
Rana P. B. Singh Banaras (Varanasi) Cosmic Order, Sacred City, Hindu Traditions
Alain Daniélou: Mythes et Dieux de l'Inde
La civilisation des différences
Approche de l'hindouisme
Maïna Kataki: Paroles de Lal Ded

SCHEME OF TRANSLITERATION

Vowels			*Consonants*		
अ	a	क	k	त	t
आ	ā	ख	kh	थ	th
इ	i	ग	g	द	d
ई	ī	घ	gh	ध	dh
उ	u	ङ	ṅ	न	n
ऊ	ū	च	c	प	p
ऋ	ṛ	छ	ch	फ	ph
ॠ	Ṛ	ज	j	ब	b
ल	ḷ	झ	jh	भ	bh
लॄ	Ḷ	ञ	ñ	म	m
ए	e	ट	ṭ	य	y
ऐ	ai	ठ	ṭh	र	r
ओ	o	ड	ḍ	ल	l
औ	au	ढ	ḍh	व	v
		ण	ṇ	श	ś
				ष	ṣ
				स	s
				ह	h

श्र śra   क्ष kṣa   ज्ञ jña   त्र tra

Visarga (:) ḥ   Anusvār (.) ṁ

OTHER BOOKS ON VARANASI
FROM PILGRIMS PUBLISHING

www.pilgrimsbooks.com

For Catalog and more Information Mail or Fax to:

PILGRIMS BOOK HOUSE

Mail Order, P. O. Box 3872, Kathmandu, Nepal
Tel: 977-1-4700919 Fax: 977-1-4700943
E-mail: mailorder@pilgrims.wlink.com.np